Böcker av Eric Ericson:

Design for impact, Laurence King Publishing, 2002
Brev till samhället, Kartago Förlag, 2003
Panorama, Kartago Förlag, 2005
Brev till utlandet, Kartago Förlag, 2006
To Mr Cheng, Kartago Förlag, 2008
Axel Einar Hjorth: möbelarkitekt, Signum/Atlantis Förlag 2009
Palmyra, Journal Förlag 2009
Brev till Clara och Tyra från Eric Ericson, Kartago Förlag 2009
Så fungerar samhället, Kartago Förlag 2009

Brev till utlandet
© Eric Ericson 2006
Kartago Förlag
Box 17223
104 62 Stockholm
www.kartago.se
Tryck: Norhaven A/S, Danmark, november 2009

ISBN: 97891 89632 493

Brev till utlandet

Vi vill inte vara ensamma i universum. Det måste finnas något annat intelligent liv bland alla stjärnor. Under 40 år har människan skickat ut radiosignaler i rymden i hopp om att någon därute ska svara. Redan i början av 1800-talet föreslog den tyske matematikern Carl Gauss att vi skulle plantera barrträd och spannmål på ett sådant sätt att det formade en illustration av Pythagoras sats i jätteformat. De skulle planteras på ett väldigt landområde i Sibirien så att invånarna på planeten Mars kunde se det med kikare.

År 1899 prövade Nikola Tesla på att sända ut starka radiosignaler mot rymden från sitt laboratorium och han lyckades faktiskt fånga in okända signaler. Man tror idag att det rörde sig om atmosfäriska störningar.

Sedan 1960 sänder vi ut mer organiserade radiovågor och har konstant ett radioteleskop igång som lyssnar av åtta miljoner kanaler samtidigt. Under dessa 40 år har man snappat upp en liten mängd signaler som måste ha kommit någonstans från de centrala delarna i vår galax. Den märkligaste signalen registrerades den 15:e augusti 1977, i radiobruset av ettor och nollor uppenbarade sig plötsligt en oförklarlig signal: 6EQUJ5. Efter någon minut försvann signalen lika spårlöst som den dykt upp och man har inte lyckats hitta den igen. Var det Gud som gäckade oss människor – en minut på 40 år?

Precis på samma sätt har Eric Ericson skickat ut brev till jordens befolkning, han har postat drygt 6000 brev. Brev som med sina märkliga funderingar sticker ut i det allmänna mediabruset.

Många gånger får han svar, trots att han ofta vänder på logiken och berör djupare frågor än vad det på ytan kan se ut som; han skriver att det är viktigt att inte ge dubbla budskap till djur, han undrar varför chokladtillverkaren har lagt ett spelkort i kartongen, han är oroad för att hans son röker corn flakes, han vill besöka centralbanken i Österrike med 19 mimdansare och de kommer på torsdag, han vänder sig till en tvålfabrikant i Kina som erbjudit sig att skapa en tvål som går att äta, han undrar om en frikyrka i London kan hjälpa honom att viga sina husdjur.

Vi har samlat Eric Ericsons korrespondens till världen i denna bok, som samtidigt är en uppföljare till hans tidigare succé »Brev till samhället«. Eric Ericson får ofta fantastiska svar på sina brev och ibland får han svar som leder vidare i kommunikationen mellan två världar – mellan två människor.

Rolf Classon

Dear Sir or Madam
How much pet food can a person eat before it gets
dangerous? Or can you eat as much as you want? I'm
starting to get worried so answer quickly!

Kindly regards

Eric Ericson
Mailbox 412
Birger Jarlsgatan 39
111 45 Stockoholm
Sweden

Eric Ericson
Mailbox 412
Birger Jarlsgatan 39
111 45 Stockholm
Sweden

Harderwijk, 16 december 2005

Dear Mr. Ericson,

Yarrah, the healthy and organic dog and cat food is suitable for any dog or cat.

Referring to your letter I received from you 14 December 2005 I could inform you that Yarrah Organic <u>Petfood</u> is not intended for human consumption.

We hope to have been of good service.

Kind regards,
Yarrah Organic Petfood BV

...rah Organic Pet Food is de handelsnaam en een product van Vink Sales B.V., A. van Leeuwenhoekstraat 26, P.O. Box 448, 3840 AK,
...derwijk, Holland, Tel +31 (0) 341 43 98 50, Fax +31 (0) 341 43 98 70, Bank: ABN AMRO Harderwijk 49.06.98.662, Gironr. ABN AMRO: 55.099,
...K. Harderwijk nr. 08077073, BTW nr. NL 8066.14.468.B.01, Inschrijfnr. verkoop- en leveringsvoorwaarden Vink Sales B.V., A.R. te Zutphen
...r nummer: 19/2001. Inschrijfnr. inkoopvoorwaarden Vink Sales B.V., A.R. te Zutphen onder nummer: 18/2002.

Hello

Thanks for your letter. It made me sad that I
didn't get an answer to my question, but it
cheered me up to see the dog and cat on your
letterhead. Who do those animals belong to? I
asked whether it was dangerous to eat pet food.
Or if it was ok for a person to eat as much as
he wanted? You answered that the food isn't
produced for people. So I have to ask again. Is
it dangerous to eat your food? If it is, something should be mentioned on the packaging.
You ought to have a warning label just like the
ones on cigarette packages. Can my consumption
of your products affect me?

Sincerely,

Eric Ericson
Mailbox 412
Birger Jarlsgatan 39
111 45 Stockoholm
Sweden

YARRAH ORGANIC
PET FOOD

Eric Ericson
Mailbox 412
Birger Jarlsgatan 39
111 45 Stockholm
Sweden

Harderwijk, 5 januari 2006

Dear Mr. Ericson,

Referring to your letter I received from you today I could inform you that Yarrah Organic <u>Pet-food</u> is not intended for human consumption.

Pet food is not dangerous for human. But it is not very nourishing and it is not complete for humans. It contains to much protein en to less carbohydrates. So: as long as you varied it with other food it is harmless.

We hope to have been of good service.

Kind regards,
Yarrah Organic Petfood BV

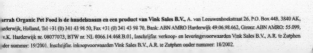

Yarrah Organic Pet Food is de handelsnaam en een product van Vink Sales B.V., A. van Leeuwenhoekstraat 26, P.O. Box 448, 3840 AK, Harderwijk, Holland, Tel +31 (0) 341 43 98 50, Fax +31 (0) 341 43 98 70, Bank: ABN AMRO Harderwijk 49.06.98.662, Giro nr. ABN AMRO: 55.099, v.K. Harderwijk nr. 08077073, BTW nr. NL 8066.14.468.B.01, Inschrijfnr. verkoop- en leveringsvoorwaarden Vink Sales B.V., A.R. te Zutphen onder nummer: 19/2001. Inschrijfnr. inkoopvoorwaarden Vink Sales B.V., A.R. te Zutphen onder nummer: 18/2002.

Hello

Like many other girls, my daughter looks up to Britney Spears as an idol and role model. For her birthday, she has one wish; that we should perform plastic surgery on her favorite dog Misha to make her look more like Britney Spears. I wonder if this is possible, and if so, how much would it cost? I also wonder how long it would take. I would like to receive more information about cost and procedure.

Best wishes

Eric Ericson
Mailbox 412
Birger Jarlsgatan 39
111 45 Stockoholm
Sweden

Mid Hudson Plastic Surgery Center
117 Marys Ave Suite 204
Kingston, N.Y 12401
Phone 845-338-0789
www.doctorofplasticsurgery.com

November 16, 2005

Eric Ericson
Mailbox 412
Birger Jarlsgatan 39
111 45 Stockholm
SWEDEN

Dear Eric,

I am in receipt of your letter requesting information on Plastic Surgery for your dog. Although Dr. Hagerty cannot perform surgery on a dog, I can give you information on Plastic Surgery for humans.

The doctor's fee for a breast augmentation would be $4500.00. The hospital and anesthesia fees would be approximately $1360.00. The total cost would be approximately $5860.00.

I am enclosing a brochure on the Breast Augmentation procedure. Please fee free to contact us again if you require any more information.

Sincerely,

,M.D.

AF SILVFERHUFVUD

Dear Sir

I'm contacting you on behalf of the Af Silvferhufvud family.
The head of the house, General Lieutenant Jan af Silfverhufvud
looking for a scent. I would like to know if you are able to manufacture a perfume with the essence of ghost, flute and dice?

Kindly regards

Eric Ericson

MCPL INDIA PRIVATE LIMITED

REGISTERED OFFICE : CMM Building, Rua de Ourem, Panjim, Goa - 403 001, India.
Tel (91) (832) 2420282, 2423860, 2431978, 2426326
Fax : (91) (832) 2423871 • E-Mail: tellmcpl@ttml.co.in

17th April 2006

To:
Mr. Eric Ericson,
AF Silverhufvud
Mailbox 412,
Birger Jarlsgatan 39,
<u>111 45 STOCKHOLM,</u>
<u>SWEDEN</u>

Dear Mr. Ericson,

Acknowledge with thanks your letter.

Yes we can manufacture perfume similar to ghost, flute and dice.

We can make them in any format that you may require i.e. EDT, EDP, or any aerosol body sprays. Please do let us know your requirement.

Please also let us know whether you will supply us the designs, packaging material or you would like us to source everything from here.

Depending on the quantity you would like us to supply will depend our price of the total arrangements you would like to get into.

Look forward to your favourable response.

Kind regards,

Yours sincerely,
For MCPL INDIA PVT LTD

Managing Director

MARKETING OFFICE : Elco Arcade, A-17, 1st Floor, 46 Hill Road, Bandra (West) Mumbai - 400 050
Tel: (91) (22) 26553102, 26404516, 26404576 • Fax : (91) (22) 26553101

Dear Sir or Madam

Recently, I met a person that works for you at a rock concert. I don't remember what his name was. It was something common, Jim or John or something. In any case, I told him that I was a mime artist and that I travel around the world miming for peace. He thought that sounded really exciting and promised that I could stay at your office between Dec 19 – Jan 16. I'm used to really simple accommodations. so it's totally ok for me to sleep in a conference room, for example, if you clear out the furniture. I have my own sleeping bag, so you don't need to worry about beddings. I also want to mention that I only eat vegetarian food. Let me know if there's anything more you need to know.

Take it easy

Eric Ericson
Mailbox 412
Birger Jarlsgatan 39
111 45 Stockoholm
Sweden

December 1, 2005

Hello Eric.

I don't know for who you send
the letter but it arrivel to me
by mistake.
I work in bank leumi in Israel,
So i send to you back the letter.

best luck for the coming

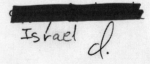

Israel d.

Hello

Thanks for your letter. There must have been some kind of misunderstanding, the man I talked with had a really common name like John or Jim or something. Is there someone at your office who is about 5'2" tall, with kind of large feet and really good at magic tricks? He had apparently been a sailor before he started working at the bank. Do you know who I mean? Or can it be someone at another bank? Are there any other banks in the area with a similar sounding name? The thing is, I loaned this guy some money and he promised he would pay me back. Are you sure that he doesn't work there at your bank and you're not just messing with me? Please get back to me as soon as you can!

Kind regards,

Eric Ericson
Mailbox 412
Birger Jarlsgatan 39
111 45 Stockoholm
Sweden

Dear Mr. Ericson

I'm sorry that I can't help
you any more.
Israel is a big country, and
ther is alot of bank
I didn't find any one whit your
 description.

hope u will find him soon.

לאומי
leumi

בנק לאומי לישראל בע״מ

Regarding the Exchange Program

On February **23** th, **17** Rumanian laborers will arrive at your place of business to bake bread. The purpose of this exchange program is to create closer con-
nections between workers in the European Union and the
former eastern block countries. You will be compensat-
ed with 1 Euro per person, per work day. The project
will continue for 7 months. The project is implemented
and finane d by a variety of EU entities, national
cooperatives, departments within a variety of sec-
tors and certain local factions within the EU in collaboration with the former eastern block states. If
you aren't able to participate, you must contact the
project leader below at the latest 4 weeks before the
project's start date. We would also like to take the
opportunity to thank you for being a part of the European Union.

Regards

EU Center for national workforce exchange,
Northern Office
Mailbox 412
Birger Jarlsgatan 39
111 45 Stockoholm
Sweden

EU Centre for National Workforce Exchange
Northern Office
Mailbox 412
Birger Jarlsgaton
111 45 Stockholm
Sweden

The Beigel Shop
155 Brick Lane
London
E1 6SB

23rd January '06

Dear Mr Ericson

RE: The Exchange Program

Thank you for your opportunity for the Romanian Labourers to take part in our business to bake bread. I am sorry we will not be able to help in any way for the Labourers to bake bread in our Bakery as it is not convenient at this time.

I apologise for not being able to co-operate with this project any further.

Kind Regards

The Beigel Shop

Dear Sir or Madam

My children heard from one of their teachers that you actively support different communist and militant groups, as well as guerilla activities around the world. At first, we felt angry and disappointed and decided that we would avoid your products. But after the first shock wore off, we discussed the matter as a family and changed our opinion. We have instead chosen to buy your products whenever possible, so that you can continue the work you do and support these groups. We would really like to hear more about it. We looked at your website but couldn't find any information. We want to know if it's possible for you to send over a brochure or any other information you have on this?

Please send stickers too, if you have any.

Regards,

Eric Ericson
Mailbox 412
Birger Jarlsgatan 39
111 45 Stockoholm
Sweden

The Goodyear Tire & Rubber Company

Consumer Relations
Akron, Ohio 44316-0001

January 17, 2006

Eric Ericson
Mailbox 412
Birger Jarlsgatan 39
111045 Stockoholm,
SWEDEN

Dear Eric:

It is unfortunate that your childrens teacher(s) is souninformed.

We see no need to defend ourselves with such alligations.

Please enjoy the stickers

Dear Sir or Madam

Tomorrow will be two months since I've stopped feeding my pets ordinary pet food. Now I give them only toothpaste and vitamin supplements. In the beginning the animals were very angry with me, but then they understood that I only wanted what was the best for them. Since then, they've been happy. I've also changed my diet a week ago and stopped eating normal food. My diet now consists of your toothpaste and different vitamin supplements. I feel better than I have in years. My animals and I are living proof of the extremely high quality of your products. That's why I think it would be appropriate to include me and my animals in your marketing campaign. It would benefit everyone involved. I'm also going to set up a webpage on the internet with pictures of me and my pets. I would also appreciate it if you could show pictures of me and my pets on your toothpaste packaging.

Kindly regards

Eric Ericson
Mailbox 412
Birger Jarlsgatan 39
111 45 Stockoholm
Sweden

GlaxoSmithKline

Eric Ericson
Mailbox 412
Birger Jarlsgatan 39
111 45 Stockholm
SVERIGE

GlaxoSmithKline
Consumer Healthcare A/S

Lautruphøj 1-3
DK-2750 Ballerup

Tel. +45 44 86 86 86
Fax +45 44 86 86 87
www.gsk.com

2005-12-05

Regarding toothpaste

We refer to the letter we received from you regarding our toothpaste. In this letter you wrote the following:

"Tomorrow will be two months since I've stopped feeding my pets ordinary pet food. Now I give them only with toothpaste and vitamin supplements"

"I've also changed my diet a week ago and stopped eating normal food. My diet now consists of your toothpaste and different vitamin supplements"

All our toothpaste contains fluoride, with a maximum concentration of 1450 ppm Fluoride. (The maximum allowed level of fluoride in toothpaste is 1500 ppm Fluoride). The toothpaste is intended to be used for cleaning the teeth **and not to be ingested, as high level of ingested fluoride can be toxic to the body. We highly recommend that you do not ingest the toothpaste or feed your pets with it.**

Kind regards

GlaxoSmithKline
Consumer Healthcare A/S

Regulatory Associate

Hello

Thanks for your letter. My animals and I feel really great from eating tooth-paste and haven't felt any negative effects. I was wondering if you knew of another kind of toothpaste that isn't dangerous to eat? I also wonder how it's possible to sell something that's dangerous? In that case, there ought to be some kind of warning on the packaging that says the product contains poison. I also wanted to ask again if you would like to have pictures of me and my animals on your packaging?

Kind regards,

Eric Ericson
Mailbox 412
Birger Jarlsgatan 39
111 45 Stockoholm
Sweden

Eric Ericson
Mailbox 412
Birger Jarlsgatan 39
111 45 Stockholm
SVERIGE

GlaxoSmithKline
Consumer Healthcare A/S

Lautruphøj 1-3
DK-2750 Ballerup

Tel. +45 44 86 86 86
Fax +45 44 86 86 87
www.gsk.com

Regarding toothpaste

We refer to the second letter we received from you regarding our toothpaste on the 16th of December 2005. In this letter you wrote the following:

"I was wondering if you knew of another kind of toothpaste that isn't dangerous to eat"

Please be aware of, as also stated in the letter we sent to you on the 5th of December 2005, that **you should not eat the toothpaste or feed your pets with it**. This refers not only to our toothpaste, but to any toothpaste which contains fluoride, as they are all intended to be used for cleaning the teeth and not to be ingested. Please be aware of that high level of ingested fluoride can be toxic to the body.

The toothpaste is not toxic or dangerous as long as it is being used as directed. Toothpaste is as stated above intended to be used for cleaning the teeth and not to be ingested. On all our toothpaste is declared that they contain fluoride.

We also need to inform you that we can not have any pictures of you and your animals on our packaging.

Please contact your doctor if you need any further information.

Kind regards

GlaxoSmithKline
Consumer Healthcare A/S

Regulatory Associate

Hello

First of all, I want to thank you so much for your invitation. I was both moved
and surprised. I had not expected it in the least. I will arrive at your place on
January 8 as agreed. I will bring approximately 200 small animals and about a
hundred midsized and large animals. You should not pet the big animals. I would
like you to order fodder for the animals right away. I have chartered a plane for
me and the animals, as this is the most effective way to transport the animals.
I have asked the airline to send the invoice to you direcetly. See you soon!

Eric Ericson
Mailbox 412
Birger Jarlsgatan 39
111 45 Stockoholm
Sweden

RiverBend Bank

November 15, 2005

Mr. Eric Ericson
Mailbox 412
111 45 Stockholm
Sweden

Dear Mr. Ericson:

I do not know anything about an invitation to you or for you to bring any animals.

We have no intention of paying for an invoice to an airline, and do not understand your letter.

Sincerely,

Chairman & C.E.O.

cc: file

Hello

Thanks for your letter. When I opened your letter I was very disappointed. First of all, I think it's very strange that you first send an invitation and then later don't want me to come. That's sending mixed messages. When you spend a lot of time near animals you quickly learn that it's dangerous to give mixed messages. There's nothing wrong with changing your mind, but you have to be very clear and come out and say it. Otherwise everyone just gets terribly disappointed. I suggest we schedule in a new time. Does January 15 work better for you? You don't need to pay for the transport of the animals. I can pay for that myself. Let me know if the date doesn't work for you.

Regards,

Eric Ericson
Mailbox 412
Birger Jarlsgatan 39
111 45 Stockoholm
Sweden

RiverBend Bank

December 12, 2005

Mr. Eric Ericson
Mailbox 412
Birger Jarlsgatan 39
111 45 Stockholm
Sweden

Dear Mr. Ericson:

I did not nor did anyone at Riverbend Bank invite you here or ask you to bring any animals. As I stated in my prior letter dated November 15, 2005, no one at Riverbend Bank knows anything about an invitation to you.

As I also stated in my prior letter to you we did not invite you here, and we have no intention of paying for an invoice to an airline, and do not understand your letter.

Sincerely,

Chairman & C.E.O.

cc: file

Dear Sir or Madam

A good friend told me to use your mustard as a facial cream. At first, I was very content with the results. I felt as if wrinkles and lines disappeared and that the skin felt younger and lighter. After using the sauce for about a month, my skin turned chappy and I developed severe rashes. In addition, I became very depressed because of the way my looks deteriorated due to the treatment. In my opinion, you should have some kind of warning label on your products, just like they do on cigarette boxes and other products hazardous to you health.

Kindly Regards

Eric Ericson
Mailbox 412
Birger Jarlsgatan 39
111 45 Stockoholm
Sweden

March 28, 2006

Eric Ericson
Mailbox 412
Birger Jarlsgatan 39
111 45 Stockholm
Sweden

Dear Eric,
We have received your letter, stating you used our Mustard product as a facial cream, based on the advice of a friend.
Our product is a condiment to be used on food. The product, is in no way meant to be used as a facial cream or lotion of any sort.
If you have any other questions or comments, please feel free to contact us.

Sincerely,

████████████ Customer Service
Plochman, Inc.

15-468-3434
15-468-8755

Plochman, Inc.
1333 North Boudreau Road
Manteno, IL 60950

www.plochman.com
Customer Service
800-843-4566

Dear Sir or Madam

In one of your packages I found this playing card. At first I got angry, then frightened and disappointed. I thought that someone was trying to trick me. I thought that maybe someone at your factory was making fun of me. That's why I got in touch with my neighbor who is a lawyer. He told me that he heard from a relative in Great Britain that you have a contest going on where people are supposed to find playing cards in your packaging. I am hereby sending in the playing card. Please send the prize to the following address as soon as possible.

Kindly regards

Eric Ericson
Mailbox 412
Birger Jarlsgatan 39
111 45 Stockoholm
Sweden

BENDICKS

9th December 2005

Mr E Ericson
Mailbox 412
Birger Jarlsgatan 39
111 45 Stockholm
Sweden

Dear Mr Ericson

Thank you for your letter.

We were most concerned to learn that you found a playing card in a box of our chocolates and would be grateful if you could return the box and chocolates to me for examination.

We are not running any competition such as you outline and appreciate that this will not allay your disappointment. Please accept our sincere apologies for the distress this matter has caused.

It will help us to investigate your findings if we know the type of chocolates (we make many varieties) and the size of the box, together with "best before" date and the production code which appears beside it. Perhaps you could also advise us as to the exact location of the playing card.

On receipt of further information we will look into this matter and be able to advise you and make recompense.

Yours sincerely
BENDICKS (MAYFAIR) LIMITED

(Mrs)
Quality Care Department

INVESTOR IN PEOPLE

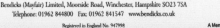
Bendicks (Mayfair) Limited, Moorside Road, Winchester, Hampshire SO23 7SA
Telephone: 01962 844800 Fax: 01962 841547 www.bendicks.co.uk
Registered in England No. 947998

A Member Of The STORCK Group

Dear ████████

I was very disappointed when I got your letter. You asked me in which product packaging I found the playing card. You ought to know. It was someone at your factory who put the playing card there. So you ought to be asking that person, the one who's trying to make a fool of me. I feel cheated. As a consumer it saddens me to buy your products and then something like this happens.

Kindly regards

Eric Ericson
Mailbox 412
Birger Jarlsgatan 39
111 45 Stockoholm
Sweden

BENDICKS®

3rd January 2006

Mr E Ericson
Mailbox 412
Birger Jarlsgatan 39
111 45 Stockholm
Sweden

Dear Mr Ericson

Thank you for responding to our letter.

Please be assured that we view your complaint seriously and wish to investigate the incident thoroughly, hence the request for the details of the product and code dates on the package. We have received no other complaint of this nature and have certainly not experienced any issues of this nature in the factory on any of the products we produce.

Very strict quality assurance procedures are in operation throughout the factory to ensure that chocolates of a consistently high standard are produced and delivered. All products are subjected to numerous quality checks, from raw materials to finished products. Each stage in the process is closely monitored by fully-trained staff. Protective clothing, headgear and beard snoods, where applicable, are worn by all personnel within the factory area and personal items are not permitted inside the production area. Lockers are provided in a designated changing area for personal items, including watches and jewellery. Food handlers are given detailed personal hygiene training before being allowed to handle food products and personal hygiene checks are carried out at the start of each shift.

We produce a range of chocolate products and require information with product type and code date from the packaging to conduct a thorough investigation and reach a satisfactory conclusion.

Yours sincerely
BENDICKS (MAYFAIR) LIMITED

Quality Care Department

INVESTOR IN PEOPLE

Bendicks (Mayfair) Limited, Moorside Road, Winchester, Hampshire SO23 7SA
Telephone: 01962 844800 Fax: 01962 841547 www.bendicks.co.uk
Registered in England No. 947998

A Member Of The STORCK Group

Dear Mrs ██████,

Thanks for your letter. The fact that you manufacture a variety of different choco-late products is no excuse. You should know who at your factories put that play-ing card there and in which package. I think it's very strange that a distinguished company like yours doesn't know what your employees are up to. You go ahead and ask your employees which package the guilty individual put that playing card in. If you aren't able to get an answer out of them, then it's possible to do forensic analysis on the playing card and compare it with your employees DNA and fin-gerprints. Then we'll see who's behind all of this. I feel discriminated against and am pretty certain that the person who put that playing card in that package is an anti-Semite and that the crime has a political or religious motive. In this day and age a lot of anti-Semites do things like that. I want you to investigate this, figure out what's really going on.

Regards

Eric Ericson
Mailbox 412
Birger Jarlsgatan 39
111 45 Stockoholm
Sweden

BENDICKS®

16th February 2006

Mr E Ericson
Mailbox 412
Birger Jarlsgatan 39
111 45 Stockholm
SWEDEN

Dear Mr Ericson

I have been shown the correspondence regarding the playing card which you found with Bendicks chocolates. I would like to add my apologies to those you have already received from Mrs Clark.

We have never experienced anything like this before. We have strict rules on what can be taken into the factory, personal belongings have to be left in lockers. We have of course asked if anyone in the factory has any knowledge, but not surprisingly no-one has come forward, anyone who would do such a thing would not admit to it, and many of the people who pack chocolates for us each year come on temporary contracts, so whoever placed the card amongst the chocolates is most likely not working here anymore. Everyone packing chocolates in our factory wears gloves, there will not be fingerprint or DNA evidence, and even if there were we would not be able to trace the temporary staff. The police would not help us as they would not regard it as a criminal offence.

So I can only offer my apologies, and an offer to refund to you the purchase price of the chocolates if you can tell us which box the card was found in and the price paid for the box.

Yours sincerely
BENDICKS (MAYFAIR) LIMITED

Managing Director

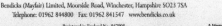
Bendicks (Mayfair) Limited, Moorside Road, Winchester, Hampshire SO23 7SA
Telephone: 01962 844800 Fax: 01962 841547 www.bendicks.co.uk
Registered in England No. 947998

Dear ████████

Thank you for your letter. As I said before, I don't intend to say in which package I found the playing card. The person who put the card there ought to have that responsibility. That you are unwilling to involve the police or take DNA samples from your employees, seems to me like an admission of guilt on your side.
If you were innocent and didn't have anything to hide, you wouldn't have anything against these investigations. I think you're hiding something. What, I don't know.

You offered me my money back for the price of the chocolates. For me, it's not a matter of money, but a matter of right and wrong. I have therefore hired a private detective to look into this case and do his own investigation. I have instructed the detective to interrogate everyone at your company so that we can get this matter cleared up. I wonder if you have anything against having the detective begin his work at your offices April 28th? If you have any concerns about this, I ask you to get in touch. The best case scenario would be if the person who placed the playing card in my chocolates would make him/herself known.

Kindly Regards

Eric Ericson
Mailbox 412
Birger Jarlsgatan 39
111 45 Stockoholm
Sweden

BENDICKS®

11th April 2006

Mr E Erickson
Mailbox 412
Birger Jarlsgatan
111 45 Stockholm
SWEDEN

Dear Mr Ericson,

Thank you for your further letter regarding the playing card.

We have nothing to hide, but as stated previously, there is no point in asking the police to investigate as no criminal act has been committed. As stated in my last letter, many of our packing staff from last year were on temporary contracts and are no longer working here, and all packing staff wear gloves. We therefore do not believe there is any benefit in looking for fingerprints or DNA evidence, so I am afraid we cannot allow a private detective to disrupt the business.

I can only apologise again to you, and offer to refund the cost of the chocolates, but beyond this I am afraid we will not enter into further correspondence.

Yours sincerely,
BENDICKS (MAYFAIR) LIMITED

Managing Director

INVESTOR IN PEOPLE

Bendicks (Mayfair) Limited, Moorside Road, Winchester, Hampshire SO23 7SA
Telephone: 01962 844800   Fax: 01962 841547   www.bendicks.co.uk
Registered in England No. 947998

A Member Of The **STORCK** Group
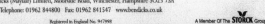

Dear Mr ███████

Thank you for your letter. I am not angry anymore. I believe the person that put the playing card in the package did it as a greeting, just like when scientists send out signals into space in hopes that a foreign civilization will receive it. In that same spirit, someone at your company sent out a playing card in one of your packages.

I want to therefore apologize. I was wrong to get angry when I didn't understand that it was some kind of message. I had a hard time in the beginning understanding that.

I've thought a lot about what the greeting means. That's why I would appreciate it if you could immediately return the playing card so I can send it off to a good friend of mine in Tel Aviv who works as a cryptologist. I'm enclosing 200 USD so that you can Fed-Ex the playing card to me.

Kindly Regards

Eric Ericson
Mailbox 412
Birger Jarlsgatan 39
111 45 Stockoholm
Sweden

BENDICKS®

5th May 2006

Mr E Erickson
Mailbox 412
Birger Jarlsgatan
111 45 Stockholm
SWEDEN

Dear Mr Ericson,

Thank you for your letter. I am glad to read that you are not angry anymore.

Please find enclosed the playing card, I am also returning the USD 200, it is not necessary for you to have to pay.

I trust this ends the matter now.

Yours sincerely,
BENDICKS (MAYFAIR) LIMITED

Managing Director

Registered in England No. 947998

A Member Of The **STORCK** Group

Dear Sir or Madam

I'm contacting you on behalf of the Af Silvferhufvud family. The family has been in possession of a dwarf since the 1970's.

The dwarf has given the family much happiness and has been much appreciated by the family's children, friends and relatives.

He has been the family's mascot ever since he was first obtained. The children have now outgrown the dwarf and he's starting to get on in years. We have therefore decided to donate the dwarf to a zoo so more people are able to get some joy out of this little creature. In Sweden the constitution does not permit zoos to be in possession of dwarfs, that is why we have chosen to contact you. The dwarf will be delivered to you February 21. If you have anything against this arrangement we ask you to get in touch with us immediately so we can contact a different zoo. We would like to thank you in advance for your help and at the same time wish you the best with our little friend. If you have any questions don't hesitate to ask.

Yours sincerely,

Eric Ericson

شركو

شركة المعادى للاستثمارات
السياحية والترفيهية

التاريخ: ..2.1.2..1.2006..

رقم القيد: ....

Mr. Eric Ericson
AF SILVFERHUFVUD
Mail box 412 , Birger Jarlsgatan 39
111 45 Stockholm , Sweden.

Dear Mr. Ericson
Thank you for your letter concerning the AF
SILVFERHUFVUD family's dwarf.
We appreciate choosing us for your donation.
We would like to have more information and
details about the dwarf and we also would like
very much to have a picture of him .
We do wish your family and the dwarf the best
of luck in finding him a place that would make
all of you happy .
We are awaiting for your prompt reply before
giving you our final opinion about accepting
your offer.

Best wishes

Eng. A.

n Towers - Above Average Housing - Building # 11, First Floor
sh El Nile - Maadi - Cairo - Egypt - Tel.:5243200 - 243300 - Fax:5243100

ابراج عثمان بالمعادى - كورنيش النيل - القاهرة - عمارة ١١ - الدور الأول - إسكان فوق المتوسط
تليفون : ٥٢٤٣٢٠٠ - ٥٢٤٣٢٠٠ - فاكس : ٥٢٤٣١٠٠ - ص . ب : ٤٧٤ المعادى

AF SILVERHUFVUD

Dear Sir

Thank you for your acceptance of the dwarf. We are all convinced that he will have a very promising future with you. I've enclosed a picture of the dwarf as you requested. He's much younger in the picture than he is today. The photo was taken approximately 8 years ago and is a copy from the family's ownership documents. These documents will be transferred over to you in connection with the delivery of the dwarf.

We have organized all the necessary documents for export to Egypt. Unfortunately, the transportation has been somewhat delayed so he won't be delivered to you until March 23. If you have any questions, you are more than welcome to contact me.

Yours sincerely,

Eric Ericson

METRICO

Maadi Touristic & Recreation
Investement Company

شركو

شركة المعادى للاستثمارات
السياحية والترفيهية

Date : ....
No. : ....

التاريـخ : 201.2.1.2006....
رقم القيد : ....

Mr. Eric Ericson
AF SILVFERHUFVUD
Mail box 412 , Birger Tarlsgatan 39
111 45 Stockholm , Sweden.

Dear Sir:-

Sorry to tell you that We can't accept the dwarf
with us. We just wanted earlier to know more
about your request without any strings attached
Again , We do clarily that We do not accept the
dwarf with us.
Thank you and best wishes for you all.

Eng. A███████████

Eng. A. Abd█

man Towers - Above Average Housing - Building # 11, First Floor
nish El Nile - Maadi - Cairo - Egypt -Tel.:5243200 - 243300 - Fax:5243100

ابراج عثمان بالمعادى-كورنيش النيل-القاهرة-عمارة١١-الدور الأول-إسكان فوق المتوسط
تليفون : ٥٢٤٣٢٠٠-٢٤٣٣٠٠-فاكس : ٥٢٤٣١٠٠ - ص.ب : ٤٧٤ المعادى

Dear Sir or Madam

A friend of mine knows a guy that spent time in England who had met someone on the train between London and Manchester. He said that you need a clown to perform at your place 6 days a week all next year. He also said that it was extremely urgent. I just wanted to say that I'll take the job. I'll come over as soon as I can. I won't be able to leave before December 4, because I'm participating in a political gala. If there's anything you need from Sweden let me know as soon as possible. Otherwise we'll see each other soon.

All the best

Eric Ericson
Mailbox 412
Birger Jarlsgatan 39
111 45 Stockoholm
Sweden

**Consulate General
Of The
Arab Republic of
Egypt**

2, LOWNDES STREET
LONDON SW1X 9ET
TEL : 020 – 7235 9777
FAX : 020 – 7235 5684

**Mr. Eric Ericson
Mailbox 412
Birger Jarlsgatan 39
111 45 Stockholm
Sweden**

Date: 25/11/2005

Dear Mr. Ericson,

Regarding your request, we would like to inform you that the information your friend has provided to you is incorrect. The Consulate provide services to Egyptian Immigrants in the UK and Tourists, but no entertainment services (Clown) are provided. We wish you good luck.

**Best Regards,
Consulate General
of the A.R.E. in London**

Dear Sir or Madam

I have participated in a contest sponsored by your company and one of your retailers. The contest offered those that succeeded in lying in a tanning bed for 24 hours a day for 30 days in a row a complete cash-back rebate on the tanning bed. I thought the contest sounded exciting and therefore bought a tanning bed. When I later went back to the store after completing the contest to get my money back, the store was gone. As a consumer, it's very disappointing to enter a competition and then something like this happens. It doesn't feel at all fun. Especially since I took four weeks off from work to lay in the tanning bed. I demand an explanation from you.

Regards

Eric Ericson
Mailbox 412
Birger Jarlsgatan 39
111 45 Stockoholm
Sweden

Dear Eric Ericson,

We haven got any agent, distributor, retailers or any contact in Sweden.
We never sold any solarium to Sweden.

Black Care Distribution Manufactoring Company.

Kelt: Budapest, 2006. április 3.

Dear Sir or Madam

My name is Eric Ericson. I'm actively working on a project engaged in and in support of getting mime dancers out into the business world. Many mime dancers don't have the resources to support themselves and have difficulties finding work. There's also the problem that a lot of companies don't like to have mimes at their offices. Mime artists are a minority group with a history of being discriminated against and can use all the help they can get. That's why I'm actively working to get mime dancers into the trade and industry workforce.

The world is controlled by money. Money is power. In the current state of affairs, there isn't a single mime dancer actively working in banking. And that's why mime dancers don't have the opportunity to influence things in our society. The mimes' voices are not being heard. That's why it's incredibly important that mime dancers get the opportunity to work in banking. So that in the long-term, mimes can get their voices heard and influence society. As long as mime dancers don't have higher positions in society and business, we are not living in a democracy.

I now have 19 unemployed mime dancers who wish to break into the business world and work in banking. They would like to work at your place of business for a 6-month trial period. I plan to come over to your office with the mime dancers January 17. I'm certain that the mime dancers and banking employees will find they have a lot to learn from each other. If you are not able to receive the group on January 17, I would be grateful if you could get back to me with a new date as soon as possible.

Regards

Eric Ericson
Mailbox 412
Birger Jarlsgatan 39
111 45 Stockoholm
Sweden

Eric Ericson
Mailbox 412
Birger Jarlsgatan 39
111 45 Stockholm
Sweden

28.12.2005/jrs/hls

Dear Mr. Ericson,

we would like to thank you for your letter from the 21" of December, addressed to our company the Raiffeisen Zentralbank Österreich AG, within you present your project "mime dancers".

The project you outlined sounds interesting, but as a matter of fact, RZB is concentrating mainly on certain Austrian institutions, according to the focus of our communication and strategic alignment. Therefore we would appreciate your kind understanding that RZB could not act as a member in this concrete project.

According to your plan to visit in Vienna on Tuesday, January 17th, 2006, as well as your wish to find for the unemployed mime dancers a work at our place we have to renounce.

With kind regards
RAIFFEISEN ZENTRALBANK ÖSTERREICH
AKTIENGESELLSCHAFT

Raiffeisen Zentralbank Österreich AG A-1030 Wien • Am Stadtpark 9 • Telefon +43-1-71707-0 • Fax +43-1-71707-1715 • Internet http://www.rzb.at
Postanschrift A-1011 Wien • Postfach 50 • Telex 136989 • Sitz der Gesellschaft in Wien • Registriert unter FN 58882t beim Handelsgericht
Wien • UID ATU 15349308 • DVR 0030961 • Swift Code RZBA AT WW • Bankleitzahl (BLZ) 31000 • Mitglied der Unica Bankengruppe

Dear ▮▮▮▮▮▮▮

I was very disappointed when I received your letter. The mime dancers were even MORE disappointed. They feel insulted. One of the artists has refused to eat since we received the letter. They looked forward to this so much. I wonder if we can come by February 7 to talk about this and figure out what went wrong? I think the mime dancers would appreciate this courtesy very much. It would also give you the opportunity to meet the mimes, and that in itself could probably get you to change your minds. I suggest that we meet at your office 10am, February 7. If there are any problems, please let us know.

Sincerely,

Eric Ericson
Mailbox 412
Birger Jarlsgatan 39
111 45 Stockoholm
Sweden

Eric Ericson
Mailbox 412
Birger Jarlsgatan 39
111 45 Stockholm
Sweden

09.01.2006/jrs/fse

Dear Mr. Ericson,

we have received your reply to our letter from the 28th of December 2005 concerning your project "mime dancers".

We have to confirm our negative reply by the mentioned reasons that RZB chiefly supports Austrian institutions due to our communication and strategic alignment. We hope you will understand our maintained standpoint.

In that case we also renounce to your recommended appointment on Tuesday, February 7th, 2006.

With kind regards
RAIFFEISEN ZENTRALBANK ÖSTERREICH
AKTIENGESELLSCHAFT

Raiffeisen Zentralbank Österreich AG A-1030 Wien • Am Stadtpark 9 • Telefon +43-1-71707-0 • Fax +43-1-71707-1715 • Internet http://www.rzb.at Postanschrift A-1011 Wien • Postfach 50 • Telex 136989 • Sitz der Gesellschaft in Wien • Registriert unter FN 58882i beim Handelsgericht Wien • UID ATU 15349308 • DVR 0030961 • Swift Code RZBA AT WW • Bankleitzahl (BLZ) 31000 • Mitglied der Unica Bankengruppe

Regarding the cancellation of business training for mimes

Thanks for your letter. We have a person from India among our mime performers. He feels really bad about all this and is convinced that it is due to racial discrimination that you don't want the mimes to come. He blames himself for the cancellation which has lead to a split within the group. We want to know if it was due to racial discrimination that made you decide not to allow us to come? We just want to be sure what's going on so we can put an end to this correspondence.

Sincerely,

Eric Ericson
Mailbox 412
Birger Jarlsgatan 39
111 45 Stockoholm
Sweden

Eric Ericson
Mailbox 412
Birger Jarlsgatan 39
111 45 Stockholm
Sweden

17.01.2006/srj/hls

Dear Mr. Ericson,

thank you very much for your letter, which is the reply to our letter from the 9th of January 2006 concerning your project "mime dancers".

To your accusation of racial discrimination we have to state the following.

The Raiffeisen Zentralbank Österreich AG (RZB) is offering financial services to customers all over the world. After we have received your first letter in December 2005, we have consulted our personnel department, if it would be an interesting project to have mime dancers in the banking world, which was declined. According to this decision, as well as the strategic and social alignment of the RZB we have turned down your inquiry, which has nothing to do with racial discrimination.

Again we would appreciate your kind understanding that RZB cannot support your project, but we wish you all the best for your future intentions.

With kind regards
RAIFFEISEN ZENTRALBANK ÖSTERREICH
AKTIENGESELLSCHAFT

Raiffeisen Zentralbank Österreich AG A-1030 Wien • Am Stadtpark 9 • Telefon +43-1-71707-0 • Fax +43-1-71707-1715 • Internet http://www.rzb.at
Postanschrift A-1011 Wien • Postfach 50 • Telex 136989 • Sitz der Gesellschaft in Wien • Registriert unter FN 58882r beim Handelsgericht
Wien • UID ATU 15349308 • DVP 0030961 • Swift Code RZBA AT WW • Bankleitzahl (BLZ) 31000 • Mitglied der Unico Bankengruppe

The Grave of the Unknown Mimes

I have been in contact with you earlier regarding helping mimes enter
the business industry. Aside from getting mimes situated in the working
world, we are also working to build The Grave of the Unknown Mimes.
The Grave of the Unknown Mimes is a monument for all the mimes who
have passed away unable to be identified. The monument will consist
of a 430 meter high statue representing a mime dancer. High atop the
mime's hat will be a flame that burns for all the mimes that have fallen in
the line of duty. The fire will burn for 24 hours a day, seven days a week,
and 365 days a year. The flame will lead sailors, pilots, hikers, cabbies,
hobos, vehicles and convoys to the monument. The monument is antici-
pated to be finished 2010. Even relics from known mimes will be pre-
served within the monument. Each year a parade will be held in conjunc-
tion with the anniversary of the monument's completion. We are sending
you this letter because parts of the financing are still unresolved. We
wonder if you would be interested in contributing to the project? We
have built a model of the monument that is about 3 meters tall that we
would like to present to you. Is it possible for us to come by March 23th
to show the model and tell you more about the project? If it's not possible, please let us know.

Kindly regards

Eric Ericson
Mailbox 412
Birger Jarlsgatan 39
111 45 Stockoholm
Sweden

Eric Ericson
Mailbox 412
Birger Jarlsgatan 39
111 45 Stockholm
Sweden

28.02.2006/srj/hls

Dear Mr. Ericson,

thank you very much for your letter, which we received on February 28th 2006, concerning your project "The Grave of the Unknown Mimes".

As already mentioned several times, the Raiffeisen Zentralbank Österreich AG (RZB) is concentrating mainly on certain Austrian institutions, according to the focus of our communication and strategic alignment. Therefore we would appreciate your kind understanding that RZB could not act as a member in this concrete project.

According to your plan to visit in Vienna on Thursday, March 23rd 2006, at our place, we have to renounce.

Again we would appreciate your kind understanding that RZB cannot support your project, but we wish you all the best for your future intentions.

With kind regards
RAIFFEISEN ZENTRALBANK ÖSTERREICH
AKTIENGESELLSCHAFT

J. Schüsler   J. Haslinger

Raiffeisen Zentralbank Österreich AG A-1030 Wien • Am Stadtpark 9 • Telefon +43-1-71707-0 • Fax +43-1-71707-1715 • Internet http://www.rzb.at
Postanschrift A-1011 Wien • Postfach 50 • Telex 136989 • Sitz der Gesellschaft in Wien • Registriert unter FN 58882t beim Handelsgericht Wien • UID ATU 15349308 • DVR 0030961 • Swift Code RZBA AT WW • Bankleitzahl (BLZ) 31000 • Mitglied der Unico Bankengruppe

Hello

Thank you for your letter. It's a shame that you won't be able to meet with us and take a look at the model. I am enclosing instead an illustration of the monument. I hope it gives you some idea of the project, even if it's just a drawing. The monument will be built in stone.

A person we have met with recommended that we build a restaurant in the hat to increase profitability of the venture. He also suggested that we charge an entrance fee to ride to the top of the monument. We think that it could be a good idea, but we're worried that people wouldn't want to ride up to the hat if it costs money? What do you think? You work with money everyday, you must have some idea?

We would also like to take the opportunity to open an account at your bank. I'm enclosing 1000 SKR for you to deposit into an account. I would also like Roger, Miro, Zizo, Soto, Mimmi, Cirzo, Mimo Mamo and Gerard to have access to the account. I would also like to take the opportunity to ask if you know of anyone else who could finance the monument and how much do you think the construction will cost?

Kindly regards

Eric Ericson
Mailbox 412

28.3.2006/srj/hls

Dear Mr. Ericson,

Thank you for your letter, which is the reply to our letter from the 28<th> of February 2006 concerning your project "The Grave of the Unknown Mimes".

As already mentioned several times, the Raiffeisen Zentralbank Österreich AG (RZB) is concentrating mainly on certain Austrian institutions, according to the focus of our communication and strategic alignment. Therefore we would appreciate your kind understanding that RZB could not act as a member in this concrete project.

As also already mentioned the RZB is offering financial services to the Top 1,000 corporate customers of Austria, therefore we can't open a private account four you with your SEK 1,000.–. That's why we have enclosed your money to this letter.

Again we would appreciate your kind understanding that RZB cannot support your project, but we wish you all the best for your future intentions.

With kind regards
RAIFFEISEN ZENTRALBANK ÖSTERREICH
AKTIENGESELLSCHAFT

J. Sch...

Raiffeisen Zentralbank Österreich AG A-1030 Wien • Am Stadtpark 9 • Telefon +43-1-71707-0 • Fax +43-1-71707-1715 • Internet http://www.rzb.at Postanschrift A-1011 Wien • Postfach 50 • Telex 136989 • Sitz der Gesellschaft in Wien • Registriert unter FN 58882t beim Handelsgericht Wien • UID ATU 15349308 • DVR 0030961 • Swift Code RZBA AT WW • Bankleitzahl (BLZ) 31000 • Mitglied der Unica Bankengruppe

Hello

First of all, I want to thank you so much for your invitation. I was both moved and surprised. I had not expected it in the least. I will arrive at your place on January 8 as agreed. I will bring approximately 200 small animals and about a hundred midsized and large animals. You should not pet the big animals. I would like you to order fodder for the animals right away. I have chartered a plane for me and the animals, as this is the most effective way to transport the animals. I have asked the airline to send the invoice to you direcetly. See you soon!

Eric Ericson
Mailbox 412
Birger Jarlsgatan 39
111 45 Stockoholm
Sweden

Spółdzielcza Grupa Bankowa
Bank Spółdzielczy w Toruniu
87-100 Toruń, ul. Reja 23c
tel. (0-56) 658-04-04, fax 658-04-14

Torun, 09.11.2005

Ldz. 3771/2005

Dear Sir,

Regarding to the mail, concerning your visit in Torun (Poland), I inform you, as following:

1. We don't know you,
2. We have never invited you to Poland,
3. We do only deal with banking business – not with animals,
4. We don't expect you and especially your 300 animals,
5. We will not pay any invoice received from airline.

Best regards,

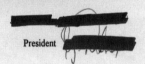

President

Dear Sir or Madam

Enclosed within is the plaing card as per agreement. Please send the prize to the address below.

Kindly regards

Eric Ericson
Mailbox 412
Birger Jarlsgatan 39
111 45 Stockoholm
Sweden

KANSAS LOTTERY

April 10, 2006

Mr. Eric Ericson
Mailbox 412
Birger Jarlsgatan 39
111 45 Stolkholm
Sweden

Dear Mr. Ericson:

The Kansas Lottery is in receipt of your undated letter and "2 of hearts" playing card (both of which I am returning to you herewith). The Kansas Lottery has absolutely no idea to what you may be referring in your letter, we do not now and have never had any such promotion or giveaway, and we have no prize to offer you based upon said letter. We certainly hope you have not fallen victim to some sort of scam or other fraud.

Thank you.

Sincerely,

Assistant Attorney General
Kansas Lottery

: letter and playing card
Director of Security, Kansas Lottery

Dear ▇▇▇▇▇

Thank you for your letter. I talked with Roger who originally told me that I should send the playing card to you. He told me that I should return the playing card, along with a penalty-fee of 20 USD for not having returned the card before the turn of the new year. If I didn't, I would be obligated to pay the prize amount to the next lotto winner and that would be financially unfeasible for me. He also said that I should request a receipt from you to show that you've received the money.

Kindly regards

Eric Ericson
Mailbox 412
Birger Jarlsgatan 39
111 45 Stockoholm
Sweden

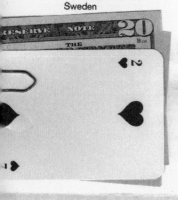

KANSAS LOTTERY

May 3, 2006

Mr. Eric Ericson
Mailbox 412
Birger Jarlsgatan 39
111 45 Stolkholm
Sweden

Dear Mr. Ericson:

The Kansas Lottery has received the second of your two undated letters, along with a $20US bill, and the same "2 of hearts" playing card I returned to you in my letter of April 10, 2006. Again, the Kansas Lottery has absolutely no idea to what you may be referring in your letter, we do not now and have never had any such promotion or giveaway, and we have no prize to offer you based upon said letter. I am returning herewith the playing card and $20 bill.

There is no need to send anything further to the Kansas Lottery regarding this matter. If we do in fact receive any further items or correspondence, they probably will not be returned as postage to Sweden is rather expensive and I have a duty to the Kansas Lottery and State of Kansas to preserve state assets. Please do NOT send anything further to this office pertaining to this matter.

Thank you.

Sincerely,

Assistant Attorney Gene
Kansas Lottery

encls: playing card and $20 bill
cc: ▮▮▮▮▮ Director of Security, Kansas Lottery

SAMIR

My name is Eric Ericson and I represent Mr. Samir.

In the beginning, Samir was a mime dancer and crystal therapist, but seven years ago he was abducted by a UFO and disappeared for nearly 2 years. All of his friends thought that something had happened to him when they hadn't heard from him for such a long time. When Samir came back he had attained knowledge that no other earthly person possess. Samir had learned how to change the flow of energy through working with different colors.

Many people today work in offices and think that it's a monotone environment that isn't conducive to development. Office environments are often sterile environments that don't develop individual individuality. Samir will therefore come and repaint your whole office, including the furniture. He will work with brilliantly bright, spiritually optic colors. For short periods of time, the electricity will stop working. In order for Samir to feel the energy flow, sometimes the power must be shut off and certain cables rerouted. The work will take about 2-3 weeks, so everyone should be mentally prepared for that. When the work has been completed Samir will tell about how he was taken against his will to the UFO and how he later came back with his wisdom. The lecture will conclude with Thomas Ohlsson playing the drums, those that want to can feel free to dance. If you want to give Samir a gift or money, you can give him cash or checks made out to Samir after the lecture. Samir also accepts major credit cards. If you give Samir money via credit card a 3% service tax will be applied. Samir will begin work at your office February 14. If you would like to change the date, you'll need to let us know three weeks prior. I also want to mention that Mr. Samir only eat vegetarian food.

Mr. Samir and all the rest of us who work at Samir Energy Centra look forward to meeting you!

Eric Ericson

ert Solicitors
Weston Street
don Bridge
don
3RS

Telephone
020 7234 0707
Facsimile
020 7234 0909

mail@calvertsolicitors.co.uk
www.calvertsolicitors.co.uk

FAO Eric Ericson
Mailbox 412
Birger Jarlsgatan
11 45 Stockholm
Sweden

Our Ref: NDC/jb/Samir

By Post

5 January 2006

Dear Sir,

Re: Mr Samir

We write in reply to your undated letter received by us on 3 January 2006 to confirm that
we have no interest in Mr Samir's services and refuse his offer to work at our offices.

Yours faithfully,

Calvert Solicitors

Partners
Nigel Calvert - Principal
Michael Hartley

Solicitor
John Bentham

Trainees
Sajjad Khan
Tinu Adeshile

Consultants
David Kenyon
Shakeel Aktar

Paralegal
Doretta Dunkley

Calvert Solicitors
is regulated by
The Law Society

SAMIR

Dear Sir or Madam

I'm contacting you regarding your letter concerning MR Samir dated January 5, 2006. We've rescheduled the appointment for March 7, 2006. We hope the date is more accommodating to you, if not, let us know.

Mr. Samir and all of us who work with him at Samir Energy Centra look forward to meeting you!

Kind regards,

Eric Ericson

lvert Solicitors
Weston Street
ndon Bridge
ndon
1 3RS

Telephone
020 7234 0707
Facsimile
020 7234 0909

mail@calvertsolicitors.co.uk
www.calvertsolicitors.co.uk

FAO Eric Ericson
Mailbox 412
Birger Jarlsgatan
111 45 Stockholm
Sweden

Our Ref: NDC/jb/Samir

By Post

25 January 2006

Dear Sir,

Re: Mr Samir

We write further to our letter of 5 January in reply to your undated letter received by us on 25 January 2006.

We again confirm that we have **<u>absolutely no interest</u>** in Mr Samir's services and refuse his offer to work at our offices in any way and on any date.

We will not enter into any further correspondence with you.

Yours faithfully,

██████████████

Calvert Solicitors

Partners
Nigel Calvert - Principal
Michael Hartley

Solicitor
John Bentham

Trainees
Sajjad Khan
Tinu Adeshile

Consultants
David Kenyon
Shakeel Aktar

Paralegal
Doretta Dunkley

Calvert Solicitors
is regulated by
The Law Society

Dear Sir or Madam

I have been working intensely for many years ministering to my animals in the name of Christ our Lord and Savior. The animals have already learned to appreciate Christian values in a spontaneous and natural way. The next step for the animals now is to enter into a holy union so that they will be able to fornicate without sinning in the eyes of God. It's for that reason I would like my animals to be married by the church. I want the wedding to be beautiful, a storybook wedding. I will be coming to the church January 18 with the animals. If there are any problems please contact me.

Christian blessings,

Eric Ericson
Mailbox 412
Birger Jarlsgatan 39
111 45 Stockoholm
Sweden

CHURCH of CHRIST the KING

46, Lakedale Road
Plumstead
London
SE18 1PS

Tel: 020-8854-0688
Email: office@cckse.com
www: cckse.com

6 November 2005

Reg. Charity No. 294196

Dear Eric,

Thank you for your letter received 14th November 2005. However, **I regret to inform you that we are unable to facilitate your request,** nor are we able to entertain any further correspondence in this matter.

Kind regards,

MIRZLANDA
INVEST

Dear Sir or Madam

I am contacting you on behalf of my client. I've been assigned by a leading tobacco company to find an advertising agency suitable to their needs for launching and marketing a new, lucrative tobacco product. Hence this letter.

Over the past few years the tobacco company has lost huge profits on account of the reduction in tobacco smoking. The tobacco company is now searching for attractive new target groups and markets both globally and locally. My client has unveiled an exciting premium product aimed at household pets. The product will be launched in select countries in Africa/Asia in September 2006.

The assignment involves producing packaging and an image campaign focused on appealing to pets and owners of household pets. The focus is to shape a trend among pet owners to indulge their pets with something extra and create a positive spin for tobacco smoking among animals. If you really love your pets, you'll pamper them with this premium product.

The campaign should work both outdoors on billboards and at point-of-purchase displays in supermarkets and boutiques, as well as the internet.

The campaign will be launched in Africa/Asia September 2006, that's why it's important for us to make a decision on our marketing collaborator right away. If you have experience with both the pet food industry and marketing of tobacco products, my employer sees that as a plus.

We would like to know more about your experience and if you would be interested in the assignment. We would like a written response from you as soon as possible.

Sincerely,

Eric Ericson

Dear Mr. Eric Erickson

It gives us honor to be one of the candidates companies for your campaign concerning packing tobacco product and make advertising campaign in Africa and Asia.

We are willing through 15 years of experience in the advertising field in (Outdoor, Indoor, tv, print media) to plan your advertising campaign with the highest level.

In case of choosing our agency to make your campaign, there are some questions to begin our steps for this campaign:

- We would like to know more about your product and who are the competitor concerning quality, price, distribution and advertising.

- The African and Asian aimed countries for this campaign.

- The suggested budget for the advertising campaign.

To know more about our business please visit our website

www.africa-advertising.net

Marketing Manager

Dear Sir or Madam

As a consumer I am both saddened and disappointed to find out on the internet that the eagle you use in your logo is a Nazi eagle. It's horrible how an organization like yours can subliminally support Nazism. I would very much like an explanation to why you use a Nazi eagle?

Kindly regards

Eric Ericson
Mailbox 412
Birger Jarlsgatan 39
111 45 Stockoholm
Sweden

AmericanAirlines®

December 14, 2005

Mr. Eric Ericson
Birger Jarlsgatan 39
Mailbox 412
Stockoholm
SWEDEN 11145

Dear Mr. Ericson:

I am in receipt of your recent letter, and I appreciate the time you took to send us your comment about the eagle we use in our logo. While you didn't send any printed examples of the comparison you made, I was not able to locate any American Airlines 'logo eagle' that resembled anything used by Nazis, past or present. I can assure you that American Airlines has absolutely no support for such ideology, subliminally or otherwise, and we distance ourselves from your suggestion.

Nevertheless, it is helpful for us to consider such matters from our customers' perspective, and you can be sure that managers in our marketing and advertising departments are reviewing your comments. As we place your observation under further review, I thank you for giving us the benefit of your opinion.

Sincerely,

Dear Sir or Madam

I had contact with you earlier regarding a delivery, but I forgot who at your office I had talked to before. Sometimes I have a really hard time remembering names. I don't even remember exactly what we agreed upon. The only thing I remember was that I, apart from payment for the delivery, was supposed to bring a bunch of animals to your office that we planned to grill in celebration of the delivery. I am a man of my word and intend to keep my promises. I plan to come to your place of business December 15th. I'm going to have with me enough animals to feed about 50 people. A number of the animals are bad tempered, but I have them in cages, so there's no problem as long as no one tries to pet them. We'll eat the angry first. Then after we have eaten our fill we can all pet the nice animals. I'm also going to arrange a lottery and raffle off the prettiest animals. If you want to do this another day let me know and we can decide on a new date. If I don't hear back from you, then we'll see each other the 15th of December.

Sincerely

Eric Ericson
Mailbox 412
Birger Jarlsgatan 39
111 45 Stockoholm
Sweden

BANQUE DE BRETAGNE

AGENCE DE PARIS
11 ET 13 RUE DU DEPART
75014 PARIS
Tél 0 820 887 066
Fax 01 40 64 55 33

Monsieur ERICSON Eric
Mailbox 412
Birger Jarlsgatan 39
111 45 Stockholm
99999 SUEDE

PARIS le 22/11/2005

RBL/MIL

Dear Mr ERICSON,

Please, note that I am not interested with your offer.

Sincerely

DIRECTEUR

S.A. au capital de 52.920.868 Euros - N° 549 200 491, RCS Rennes - identifiant C.E. FR31549200491
Siège Social : 18, quai Duguay-Trouin - 35084 Rennes - Télex BANOR A 730094F - Swift BDEBFR2R

Dear Sir or Madam

This is a very serious letter. It has come to my attention that my son and his friends have smoked cereals out of pipes on numerous occasions, often as they are partying. They have picked this idea up after checking out a database on the Internet. I have tried to talk to my son, explaining to him that it may be dangerous to smoke cereals. As I've tried to talk to him, he has become very aggressive. He has never behaved in such an aggressive way before. I told a colleague, an expert on the central nervous system, about what had happened. He said that he thinks that the aggressive behaviour may stem from smoking cereals. You should immediately launch an advertising campaign to stop this. As a parent, it makes you very sad, and you become very worried that Nestlé are using young people to sell more cereals, just like the tobacco companies do to young people. As we are awaiting your reply, my family and I will avoid your products.

Kindly regards

Eric Ericson
Mailbox 412
Birger Jarlsgatan 39
111 45 Stockoholm
Sweden

Nestlé & General Mills
Cereal Partners UK

Mr Eric Ericson
Mailbox 412
Birger Jarlsgatan 39
111 45 Stockoholm
Sweden

17 November 2005

Dear Mr Ericson

I am shocked and alarmed at the contents of your letter that I received today and I have passed
it to our customer relations department at our Head Office who will be in contact with you
shortly.

I can assure you that we are taking the matter extremely seriously and I thank you for bringing
it to our attention.

Yours sincerely

Factory Manager

Tel: 01707 824900   Staverton
Fax: 01707 824901   Trowbridge
                 Wiltshire
                 BA14 6PG

INVESTOR IN PEOPLE

Partners:
Nestlé UK Ltd, Registered in England No. 51491, St. George's House, Croydon Surrey CR9 1NR
General Mills North America Affiliates, (A partnership of General Mills Canada Inc. and General Mills Products

Hello

I feel that you are not taking the problem with teenagers smoking your cereals seriously enough. Several weeks have passed since I informed you of the situation and I think it is very strange that you still haven't put some kind of warning label on your packaging. I spoke with a neighbor about this problem the other day and he thinks that you as a company see this as a new market. He has a theory that you use lobbyists to create a trend among today's youth to smoke your cereals. I can understand that it's important for a large company to find new markets, but I think this is starting to go too far.

Kindly regards

Eric Ericson
Mailbox 412
Birger Jarlsgatan 39
111 45 Stockoholm
Sweden

CPUK

Nestlé & General Mills
Cereal Partners UK

Mr Eric Ericson
Mailbox 412
Birger Jarlsgatan 39
11145 Stockoholm
Sweden

9 January, 2006

Dear Mr Ericson

Thank you for your recent correspondence regarding the issue of youths smoking breakfast cereals. I am sorry to learn that you have not received our original response, and apologise for any inconvenience caused.

I would like to reassure you that we do not market our cereal for the purpose of smoking and do not have any need to introduce a warning on our packaging or launch an advertising campaign to stop this.

If someone does try smoking cereals they will also have ready access to other sources of wheat such as bread, cake or biscuits.

We do appreciate the time you have taken to notify us of your concerns, and I will ensure that the relevant personnel are informed of your findings.

Yours sincerely
For CEREAL PARTNERS UK

Consumer Affairs Manager

el: 01707 824900   Staverton
ax: 01707 824901   Trowbridge
                    Wiltshire
                    BA14 6PG

INVESTOR IN PEOPLE

Partners:
Nestlé UK Ltd, Registered in England No. 51491, St. George's House, Croydon Surrey CR9 1NR
General Mills North America Affiliates, (A partnership of General Mills Canada Inc. and General Mills Products

Dear ▬▬▬▬▬

Thanks for your letter. I felt both angry, sad and disappointed. I think that you are consciously diminishing the seriousness of the problem with adolescents smoking cornflakes or ignoring the problem completely. One of the reasons for this is surely because it's mainly black kids and minority groups who are smoking your cornflakes. Just in the same way you marketed and sold breast-milk formula to Third World countries.

I spoke about this problem with my friend Thomas Ohlsson who works actively with teenagers on questions of consumer rights, and who travels around and gives lectures at different camps. He told me then that he had also heard of this problem. He also said that people in Colombia (among other places) who have actively tried to stop the selling of your cornflakes have been threatened by paramilitary organizations.

I implore you to include a text on your packaging that addresses the issue of cornflake smoking or that you donate money to programs to inform schools and teenagers about the problem. I want you to solve the problem before it's too late. I want to know how you are going to proceed on this urgent issue?

Regards.

Eric Ericson
Mailbox 412
Birger Jarlsgatan 39
111 45 Stockoholm
Sweden

CPUK

Nestlé & General Mills
Cereal Partners UK

Mr Eric Ericson
Mailbox 412
Birger Jarlsgatan 39
11145 Stockoholm
Sweden

3rd February, 2006

Dear Mr Ericson

Thank you for your letter.

I am sorry that you feel angry and disappointed with my response, it is not my intention to diminish the seriousness of your concerns, but having taken all of your points seriously and carried out my own investigations, I can categorically confirm that breakfast cereals are not known as recreational drugs and smoking cereals would have not have a stimulant effect. I can also confirm that there are no chemicals that could be classed as addictive narcotics in cereals.

Having accessed various web sites, the only conclusion I can draw that "Cornflake" is being used as slang terminology for "Crack Cocaine". I have enclosed a document that highlights many alternative phrases for "Cannabis", which I hope you find useful.

This can also be accessed at http://cocaine.org/javacoke.html

I hope this information answers your concerns.

Yours sincerely
For **CEREAL PARTNERS UK**

Consumer Relations
Direct line 0845 6017158

el: 01707 824900 | Staverton
ax: 01707 824901 | Trowbridge
                 | Wiltshire
                 | BA14 6PG

INVESTOR IN PEOPLE

Partners:
Nestlé UK Ltd, Registered in England No. 51491, St. George's House, Croydon Surrey CR9 1NR
General Mills North America Affiliates, (A partnership of General Mills Canada Inc. and General Mills Products

Dear Sir or Madam

A good friend told me to use your peanut butter as a facial cream. At first, I was very content with the results. I felt as if wrinkles and lines disappeared and that the skin felt younger and lighter. After using the peanut butter for about a month, my skin turned chappy and I developed severe rashes. In addition, I became very depressed because of the way my looks deteriorated due to the treatment. In my opinion, you should have some kind of warning label on your products, just like they do on cigarette boxes and other products hazardous to you health.

Kindly Regards

Eric Ericson
Mailbox 412
Birger Jarlsgatan 39
111 45 Stockoholm
Sweden

Telephone: 617-389-2600 U.S.A.
Fax: 617-387-9085
EasyLink: 62918482

THE LEAVITT CORPORATION / 100 SANTILLI HIGHWAY / EVERETT, MASS. 02149-0998

April 7, 2006

Mr. Eric Ericson
Mailbox 412
Birger Jarlsgatan 39
111 45 Stockholm
Sweden

Dear Mr. Ericson:

Acknowledging your letter recently received, we are sorry that you suffered somewhat using our peanut butter for a purpose never intended by ourselves or any other manufacturer of peanut butter worldwide.

Apparently your friend has absolutely no background in dermatology. Peanut butter is recommended solely as a food to be taken internally. Of course it is universally recognized as a most healthful and nourishing food – as long as taken internally.

We hope you will continue to use the peanut butter of our manufacture for the purpose of which it was intended.

Yours truly,

THE LEAVITT CORPORATION

President

ZIRCOZ PRODUCTS

Dear Sir or Madam

One of your clients recommended that I contact you. I'm looking for a company with experience in manufacturing soap, hence this letter. I am working on unveiling a new product aimed at children. The product is a completely unique soap. The soap has a delicious scent and is even edible. The soap is pink colored and will taste like chewing gum. The purpose of the soap is to both compete with the cleaning products industry as well as within the sweets and ice cream market. The consistency is therefore very important.

I would like to know what it would cost to produce this product and the timeframe in doing so. I wonder too if you have the capacity to produce 2 million sweet-soaps this coming year and 3.5 million the following year?

I trust you will keep this under strictest confidentiality and get back to me as soon as possible.

Regards,

Eric Ericson
Mailbox 412
Birger Jarlsgatan 39
111 45 Stockoholm
Sweden

Soap with taste

wooden popsicle stick

广东省汕头市嘉妮化妆品有限公司
GUANGDONG SHANTOU JEANYS COSMETICE CO.,LTD.

地址: 广东省汕头市潮南区峡山长虹路中段704号　电话: 0754-7815188 7815189　图文传真: 7815138　邮编: 515144

Dear Mr. Eric Ericson,

Thank you fro your last mail.

Hope you have a nice day.

I am Jenny in Shantou Jeanys Cosmetic CO., Ltd. We have received your mail. Thank you for your attention to our products and your trust to us. At this moment, we can do the soap without foam.　And if you have any samples at this moment, would you mind send us a sample? If there is some products in the Market, please tell us the brand name of the sample. But in my opinion, there is no such kind of product in the market. So if you think it is OK, we will do the soap without foam for you.

And our contact information is as below, if you have any requirement, please don't hesitate to contact with us.

Best regards,

Shantou Jenays Cosmetic CO.,Ltd

ZIRCOZ PRODUCTS

Dear ███████

Thanks for your letter and your interest in producing this hybrid-product. Unfortunately I don't have any "product samples" and there isn't any similar product available on the market. This product is one-of-a-kind, and that's why it's so exciting. We have nevertheless a little technical problem to solve.

It's important that the product produces a lather when used as a soap, but not when it's eaten as ice cream. I am convinced that there is a chemical solution to this problem. I also would like to know what's your capacity and how many soaps of this kind are you able to produce in the coming year?

I would also like to take this opportunity to ask if you think its possible to produce a flavored shampoo that can be eaten as yogurt or fruit cream? My colleague Thomas Ohlsson has completed an extensive market research project and apparently there is a great need for such a product. I'm interested in beginning production as soon as possible, so I hope to hear back from you rather quickly.

Regards,

Eric Ericson
Mailbox 412
Birger Jarlsgatan 39
111 45 Stockoholm
Sweden

GUANGDONG SHANTOU JEANYS COSMETICE CO.,LTD.
地址：广东省汕头市潮南区峡山长虹路中段704号　电话：0754-7815188 7815189　图文传真：7815138　邮编：515144

Dear Eric,

Thank you for your last mail.

Hope you have a nice day.

We are very interested in cooperating with you soon.

So we will begin creating and produce for the samples soon. We will make them with foam.

If we can produce this kind of soap we may produce 5000pcs each day at least. So you may count how many we will produce one year.

We will try on designing and creating this kind of soap as you requested.

If we have any good news, we will inform you.

If you have any requirement, please don't hesitate to contact with us,

Best regards,

Shantou Jeanys Cosmetic CO.,Ltd

Dear Sir or Madam

I have 600 animals that love to be close to people. I keep some of the on leash, some in cages and some roam free. The animals are full of joy and energy.
I would like to give the animals to you as a gift. I plan to bring the animals over on January 16, if this date does not suit you, please let me know so that we can agree on a date and time.

Kindly regards

Eric Ericson
Mailbox 412
Birger Jarlsgatan 39
111 45 Stockoholm
Sweden

FLORA CO., LTD.

3-39 HASEDASHI-CHO YOKKAICHI MIE 510-0855 JAPAN
EL.81(JAPAN)-593-45-1261 FAX.81(JAPAN)-593-45-4164 e-mail hb101@e-net.or.jp www.HB-101.co.jp

To : Eric Ericson   27 Decenber 2005

There came the letter from you.
But we did not know and we did not invite you.

Please check again.
Please do not come to us.

Thank you so much.
Best regards,

FLORA CO., LTD

SAMIR KEBAB CENTER

The glory of kebab

Dear Sir or Madam

My name is Eric Ericson and I am responsible for supply purchasing at Samir Kebab Center, a full-service company within kebab manufacturing and processing of meat products. We export Kebab to many countries within Europe and outside of Europe. Samir Kebab Center's mission statement is to sell kebab meat at competitive prices to the end consumer. We are interested in buying animals from you. We buy all kinds of animals, both living and deceased, and we pay cash. Every month we will come by to pick up the animals. We have reserved a pick up time for you on the 8th of every month beginning the 8th of March. We look forward to doing business with you. If you aren't interested in a cooperation with Samir Kebab we ask you to please contact us in writing.

Regards,

Eric Ericson

THE ROYAL VETERINARY COLLEGE
UNIVERSITY OF LONDON

Eric Ericson
Samir Kebab Center
Mailbox 412
Birger Jarlsgatan 39
111 45 Stockoholm
Sweden

20th January 2006

Dear Eric

Samir Kebab Center

I would like to thank you for your recent letter, I am writing to inform you that the College is not interested in taking up your proposal.

Yours sincerely

Simply cats hotel

Your customers have recommended that we contact you. The reason for this correspondence is that we are looking for a permanent residence for a person who thinks he is a cat. The man believes himself to be a cat after waking up from a coma after a very severe accident. He has been treated at different psychiatric clinics around Europe for the past 20 years, but have been unsuccessful in helping him return to his original identity. On the contrary, it has strengthened his belief and conviction that he is a cat. There's no longer any hope to return the person in question back to his old self. The man doesn't say a word and has a form of social behavior reminiscent of a cat's. In addition, he eats only cat food and prefers the company of other cats. I want to also take the opportunity to mention that the man is in no way aggressive, unless you tease him and get him riled up. Then he can start to hiss and scratch, but otherwise he is very calm.

In any case, we have decided that the man be allowed to live among other cats for his remaining days. We're looking therefore for a cat hotel with a lot of experience who can take in this person. In Sweden it's against the law to let a person spend a long time in a cat hotel, so we have chosen to contact cat hotels outside Sweden. We plan to come over with the person Mars 17 so that he can meet your other animals and you can get a feel for the man. We'll leave him with you for a 12 week period to see how it works out. If there are any problems, feel free to contact us. Otherwise, we'll see you in Mars.

Kind regards

Eric Ericson
Mailbox 412
Birger Jarlsgatan 39
111 45 Stockoholm
Sweden

SIMPLY CATS HOTEL
39 Mine Street
Flemington, NJ 08822

February 1, 2006

Eric Ericson
Mailbox 412
Birger Jarlsgatan 39
111 45 Stockholm
Sweden

Dear Mr. Ericson,

I am writing in response to your letter regarding your *Cat Man*. I am sorry to hear of your situation, as I am sure it must be very frustrating for both you and him. Your situation is quite unusual; but I am afraid that I will **not** be able to accommodate your request to "board" your *CatMan*. It is customary to accept **only** felines. Simply Cats Hotel has rules and regulations set forth by the Board of Health, and they would not allow this to take place.

Wishing you luck in your search.

Best Regards,
Simply Cats Hotel

Simply Cats Hotel

Thanks for your letter. We understand that providing care for a person sounds like an enormous responsibility, but he's really not any more trouble to care for than an average cat. We are prepared to make it worth your while if you would be willing to care for this person for a three week trial. I would appreciate it if we could give it a try for three weeks in April? How much you would want in monetary compensation for that service?

Kindly regards,

Eric Ericson
Mailbox 412
Birger Jarlsgatan 39
111 45 Stockoholm
Sweden

SIMPLY CATS HOTEL
39 Mine Street
Flemington, NJ 08822
908-237-2287

Eric Erikson
Mailbox 412
Berger Jarlsgatan 39
11145 Stockholm
Sweden

Dear Mr. Erikson:

As I have stated in my previous letter, I cannot, nor am I willing to accept your "catman" as a boarder in my facility. I am governed by the Board of Health, the town itself, and I am not allowed to board humans. There is no amount of money that I can accept to perform this request.

This is my **final** correspondence to you regarding this matter.

Sincerely,
Simply Cats Hotel

Kurdish week

Thanks for your order. With this letter we are confirming and verifying your request for the Kurdish Culture Festival for the week of Dec 12- 18. In connection with the Kurdish week, traditional open-fire grills and folk dancing are scheduled to be held daily at your place of business. After five working days the festival will culminate in a laser light show finale. The project is financed by different groups and public entities within EU's member countries. The purpose of the project is to spread Kurdish culture in EU countries. If you have any questions or suggestions for activities, please contact the representative at the Kurdish Center at the address below at least 4 weeks prior to the reserved event. We, the organizers of the Kurdish week, look forward to bringing the festival to you.

Sincerely,

Eric Ericson
Mailbox 412
Birger Jarlsgatan 39
111 45 Stockoholm
Sweden

Mr.Eric Ericson
Mailbox № 412
Birger Jarsgatan 39
111 45 Stockholm
Sweden

Dear Mr.Eric Ericson,

Thank you very much for your letter concerning the Kurdish Culture Festival.
We are pleased to know that you pay great attention to spreading Kurdish traditions, festivals
and culture in EU countries. But we would like to advise you that we are an educational
institution and have no possibility to arrange festivals with open-fire grills and folk dancing on
the territory of the University. Besides, we have not sent you any order on arranging the festival
in January 2006.

Thank you for attention to our University.

Yours sincerely,

Head of International Department

01. 12. 2005

Regarding Kurdish week

We were all very disappointed when we read in your letter that we aren't welcome. First you order a festival, and then you cancel the festival. Thomas Ohlsson was especially disappointed. He is a mime dancer and mentally disturbed. He
was so looking forward to coming to the Ukraine. We have therefore reserved a
flight to Ukraine in the beginning of February for him. We would appreciate it if
you could take care of Thomas Ohlsson. After all the disappointment you caused
by cancelling the festival, we think it's the least you could do. Thomas Ohlsson thinks he's a cat, and we here who work with the Kurdish Festival could use
a break. He's not aggressive, but maybe a little bit stand-offish. He's believed
himself to be a cat for many years now, so he's very easy to care for. Misha will
come to pick him up at your place in the middle of June. Let us know as soon as
possible if there are any problems with these arrangements.

Sincerely,

Eric Ericson
Mailbox 412
Birger Jarlsgatan 39
111 45 Stockoholm
Sweden

Mr.Eric Ericson
Mailbox № 412
Birger Jarsgatan 39
111 45 Stockoholm
Sweden

12 January 2006

Re: Your letter regarding Kurdish week

We have received your letter and would like to remind you that **the National University of Physical Education and Sport of Ukraine is a state institution of higher education.** Hence, we do ask you not to post this sort of letters to our address.

Hope for your understanding,

Head of International Department

Dear Sir or Madam

I have a number of small mice that like to ride the train. Every mouse wants to ride the train for about 15-25 minutes. The mice want to ride in open freight cars. Each mouse wants his own car. The mice would rather the train not go too fast, but just fast enough. I would also like to photograph my little mice while they ride your train.

I'm coming January 25. If it doesn't work out, let us know. My phone is broken so I you can't call. You can send a letter.

See you in January,

Eric Ericson
Mailbox 412
Birger Jarlsgatan 39
111 45 Stockoholm
Sweden

ROCKLAND MODEL TRAIN AND TRACTION CLUB, INC.
13 Woodwind Lane
Spring Valley, NY 10977

December 28, 2005

Eric Ericson
Mailbox 412
Birger Jarlsgatan 39
111 45 Stockoholm
Sweden

Dear Mr Ericson:

The Rockland Model Train and Traction Club does not have a layout set up in a fixed place. We set up the layouts at train shows for which we receive a fee. We are not in the business of renting a hall, for which the sponsoring organization is responsible. In order to accommodate your request you would have to rent a hall in addition to the fee for setting up and operating the layout. Hall rentals are very expensive over here running to the hundreds of dollars and frequently require some kind of insurance in addition which would have to be obtained from a broker. Our fee is $150 for one layout for one day or part of a day. Furthermore, I am not sure that we could rent a hall if mice were involved. There is also the problem that you have of bringing animals into this country and the quarantine issues associated with importation of the mice. I would suggest that you contact the American embassy for the customs regulations on the latter matter..

Very Truly Yours

Dear [redacted]

My mice want to ride your train. I've spoken with the American Embassy and they said the mice can legally be imported into the US on the condition that the mice are first held in quarantine. The mice have been held in quarantine before after a trip to India. The mice don't like it, but if the mice are able to ride the train then it's worth it. That's what they told me. The costz of rental and insurance aren't a problem for me, neither is the cost of assembling the railroad. My mice love to ride trains, and they ought to do what they love. I will be going to a Christian camp with my mice and won't be able to travel as planned. I would like to reschedule to the 3rd of March. If there are any problems let me know. Otherwise we'll see each other in March.

Kind regards,

Eric Ericson
Mailbox 412
Birger Jarlsgatan 39
111 45 Stockoholm
Sweden

ROCKLAND MODEL TRAIN AND TRACTION CLUB, INC.
13 Woodwind Lane
Spring Valley, NY 10977

January 23, 2003

Eric Ericson
Mailbox 412
Birger Jarlsgatan 39
111 45 Stockoholm
Sweden

Dear Mr Ericson:

The club discussed your proposal and came to the conclusion that it put too much of a burden on our very limited resources. Therefore I must advise you that we will not help you any further.

Very Truly Yours

AF SILVERHUFVUD

Dear Sir or Madam

I'm contacting you on behalf of the Af Silverhufvud family. The Af Silverhufvud Family has for a number of generations been in possession of a giant. The giant has no legal name and has instead been referred to as The Giant by the family and the people in its immediate surroundings. The Giant has been employed in the service of carrying stone, building railways, hauling timber, the demolition of houses, the building up of monuments and other weightier occupations.

The Silverhufvud Family's operations have been recently modernized which has led to reduced employment for The Giant. It is for that reason the Family has taken the decision to donate The Giant. The Family is convinced that he can be of great service to you and that you will receive great pleasure from his presence. The Giant will be tranquilized and delivered to you by ground transport in the middle of April. I will provide you with a more precise date as the details become available.

If you for some reason wish to refuse the Silverhufvud Family's gift, please contact me with a formal written refusal as soon as possible. If the Giant is delivered to you and later determined unable to be taken into custody, you will be required to pay transport costs for the return of The Giant to Europe, which can be costly. You will also need to arrange the necessary customs forms which is a very time-consuming task. If you have any questions, don't hesitate to contact me.

Sincerely,

Eric Ericson

VALUE TRADING COMPANY
Import & Export Agents

3rd FEB., 2006

Attn: AF SILVFERHUFVUD
    Mr. Eric Ericson

Dear Sir,

Thanks for your mail delivered to us on the 1st February 2006, containing details of The Giant belonging to the Silvfercrantz family.
We read your mail and we want further clarifications on this whole proposal. We are interested in your proposal.
Is The Giant a construction firm?
Please contact us with more and clear details about The Giant donation to us.

Our full contact information is
VALUE TRADING COMPANY.
115 Okumagba Avenue
Warri, 332211, Delta State,
Nigeria.

We look forward to your soonest reply
   Sincerely

To the person responsible for programs on TV,

I want my animals to be on color-TV. My animals are
very suitable for color-TV. I have both large and
small animals for you to film. The animals that are
angry are kept in cages. The animals that are nice
have leashes or just roam free. You can pet those
ones, but not the angry animals in cages. I want
the animals to be on the TV-set March 16ht to March
22th. I'm also enclosing a playing card as payment.
If you want me to bring my own sleeping bag or if
the date is wrong let me know. I wonder also if I
should come in the afternoon or in the morning?

Eric Ericson
Mailbox 412
Birger Jarlsgatan 39
111 45 Stockoholm
Sweden

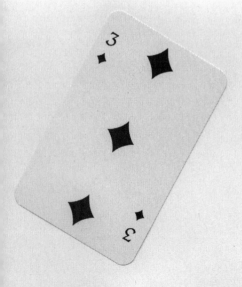

Nr 27416

Pan
Eric Ericson
Mailbox 412
Birger Jarlsgatan 39
111-45 Stockholm
Sweden

Dear Sir,

Thank you very much for your letter. We kindly inform that Polish Television can't produce any film or performance about your animals. Although we believe that your animals, both large and small, are very suitable for color-TV. But we invite you to watch our programmes and broadcasts about animals on Polish Television.

Your sincerely

REDAKTOR

Dear Sir or Madam

Your customers have recommended that we contact you. The reason for
this correspondence is that we are looking for a permanent residence
for a person who thinks he is a cat. The man believes himself to be a cat
after waking up from a coma after a very severe accident. He has been
treated at different psychiatric clinics around Europe for the past 20
years, but have been unsuccessful in helping him return to his original
identity. On the contrary, it has strengthened his belief and conviction
that he is a cat. There's no longer any hope to return the person in question back to his old self. The man doesn't say a word and has a form of
social behavior reminiscent of a cat's. In addition, he eats only cat food
and prefers the company of other cats. I want to also take the opportunity to mention that the man is in no way aggressive, unless you tease
him and get him riled up. Then he can start to hiss and scratch, but
otherwise he is very calm.

In any case, we have decided that the man be allowed to live among
other cats for his remaining days. We're looking therefore for a cat hotel
with a lot of experience who can take in this person. In Sweden it's
against the law to let a person spend a long time in a cat hotel, so we
have chosen to contact cat hotels outside Sweden. We plan to come
over with the person Mars 17 so that he can meet your other animals
and you can get a feel for the man. We'll leave him with you for a 12
week period to see how it works out. If there are any problems, feel free
to contact us. Otherwise, we'll see you in Mars.

Kind regards

Eric Ericson
Mailbox 412
Birger Jarlsgatan 39
111 45 Stockoholm
Sweden

Dear Eric Ericson:

The letter about a man who had cat spirit is quite surprising. I do not know why you select Animal Wellness Center for healing this kind of problem, however; unfortunately it is beyond our capacity/ capability to handle this case for us.

I have contacted with my higher self and God of universe about this issue. They are not agree to accept this patient since when he come to Japan, his spirit might be broken and resulted in fatal consequences. Also, our facility of Animal Wellness Center is not designed to house people, just for animals even though the man insisted as cat.

Sorry for the unexpected answer of us, however, please take care of your self and the man with cat energy. So please cancel your trip to Japan as soon as possible.

Sincerely yours

████████████, DVM,PhD

Animal Wellness Center

1-27-8 Yato Nishitokyo

Japan 188-0001

Dear Sir or Madam

I have been assigned to find a manufacturer of a new dental hygiene product for children. A lot of kids don't like to brush their teeth. This is a problem in our society. Many adults get angry at children when they don't want to brush their teeth and as a result suffer from heart problems. These heart problems cost enormous amounts of money for our society. The same goes for children with bad teeth, this is also a problem that costs society a lot of money. That is why this is an important problem to solve. The solution is to produce a toothpaste that causes kids' teeth to glow in the dark. Kids will think it's cool to brush their teeth, and adults won't suffer from heart problems to the same extent as today. A toothpaste that makes children's teeth glow in the dark would also help parents, teachers and law enforcement see which kids have not brushed their teeth. The project is financed by several EU-entities, national cooperatives, departments from within the public sector and various local factions within the EU.

The product should feel European. That is why the decision has been taken that the product ought to have a European flavor. The product's flavor will be based on the local specialties of the different countries within the EU. Each country will be entitled the submission of a local flavor based upon its representative vote within the EU-Parliament. No land will have more than 3 votes, therefore 3 flavors. The toothpaste will then be a mix of 75 total flavors, from vineyard grapes in the south to moose meat in the north. I will inform you with the exact flavor components at a later date when they have been decided. In regards to the color of the product, I can inform you that the unanimous decision has been taken that the toothpaste should be blue. The principals entrusting me with this assignment would like the product to ensure the teeth will retain their glow-in-the-dark properties for a 48 hour period after use.

I would like to know if your company has experience with and knowledge pertaining to the manufacture of such a product? Do you have the capacity to produce 1.2 million tubes of this toothpaste in 2006 with the ability to triple the production capacity the following year? The product will be launched 2006 and be sold in every EU-country. I would appreciate your written returned response as soon as possible so that we may proceed with the process.

Sincerely,

Eric Ericson

苏州福罗曼日用化学品有限公司
Suzhou fluomax daily used chemical Co.,Ltd

Dear Eric,

Thanks a lot for your kind letter.

We are Suzhou Fluo Max Daily Used Chemicals Co., Ltd., professional and serious manufacturer of toothpaste. We can produce various toothpastes and supply any flavor as you require. Our toothpaste sells all over the world, such as Australia, west European, ect. Hope we can establish a long-term business relationship with you. If you want to know more about our company, please kindly visit our web site to get more information about us.
http://fluomax.en.alibaba.com/

As you mentioned, it is a more serious issue today. It is a pleasure to cooperation with you. There is no problem of our production capacity. We have a yearly output of 50 million pieces of toothpaste. Also there is no problem with the color. You wrote *the toothpaste will be a mix of 75 total flavors.* I wonder if your meaning is that 75 kinds of toothpaste in one container. In other words, how many kinds of toothpastes do your want in one container?

I hope you also afford the following information in the next letter, such as the brand, the material of tube and the weight of toothpaste. Look forward to your favorable reply. Welcome to reply us by email. shvtrade@msn.com

Best regards!

公司地址:苏州相城区黄埭镇潘阳工业园区春秋路
ADD:Chunqiu Road,Panyang Industrial zone,Xiangcheng district,Suzhou,China
电话/TEL:0086-512-65713291, 65713282
传真/FAX:0086-512-65713286

Singapore tourism information

My wife and I are planning a trip to Singapore this summer. There are many
things in the culture to entice us, but also the sunshine and shorelines. We have a
number of acquaintances who have visited the area and have been very pleased.
There is just one thing we are worried about. Is it entirely safe to travel to Singapore? We read on the Internet that many people who have been to Singapore
have been abducted by UFOs. That is very terrifying. We would like to know
how many have suffered from this and how great a risk is it that something like
this would happen? We want to know if there are certain areas where this is more
prevalent than others? We also want to take the opportunity to ask if there are
any special places you think visitors to Singapore shouldn't miss while visiting
Singapore?

Thank you,

Eric Ericson
Mailbox 412
Birger Jarlsgatan 39
111 45 Stockoholm
Sweden

Eric Ericson
Mailbox 412
Birger Jarlsgatan 39
11145 Stockholm
Sweden

7 April 2006

Dear Mr Ericson,

Greetings from Singapore Tourism Board. I am delighted to hear of your interest in visiting Singapore and am happy to hear about the nice reports from your friends.

In answer to your question, I would have to say that not everything is true on the internet. There have been no official reports of anyone being abducted by UFOs and that the risk is next to none. I believe that Singapore is too small a country to have UFO landings and hope that this will ease your fear of being abducted.

There are many places to visit in Singapore and therefore I have also sent a few of our brochures to give you more of an idea of what places you should visit.

I hope that you have a lovely time in Singapore.

Regards

Office Adminstrator

Singapore Tourism Board
1st Floor, Carrington House, 126-130 Regent Street, London W1B 5JX, United Kingdom
Telephone: +44 (0)20 7437 0033 Facsimile: +44 (0)20 7734 2191

SAMIR KEBAB CENTER
The glory of kebab

Dear Sir or Madam

My name is Eric Ericson and I am responsible for supply purchasing at Samir Kebab Center, a full-service company within kebab manufacturing and processing of meat products. We export Kebab to many countries within Europe and outside of Europe. Samir Kebab Center's mission statement is to sell kebab meat at competitive prices to the end consumer. We are interested in buying animals from you. We buy all kinds of animals, both living and deceased, and we pay cash. Every month we will come by to pick up the animals. We have reserved a pick up time for you on the 8th of every month beginning the 8th of March. We look forward to doing business with you. If you aren't interested in a cooperation with Samir Kebab we ask you to please contact us in writing.

Regards,

Eric Ericson

UNIVERSITY OF VETERINARY MEDICINE IN KOŠICE
Komenského 73, 041 81 Košice, Slovak Republic

Košice, 30.01.2006
Č.j.:   73/R/2006

Eric Ericson
Samir Kebab Center
Mailbox 412
Birger Jarlsgatan 39
111 45 Stockholm
Sweden

Dear Mr. Ericson.

We have received your offer. It seems interesting to us, but your offer is very general, so we
e not able to declare to this thing.
e would be very glad, if we could to arrange a meeting or if you could to send us a price list –
fer, according to sort of animals, their weight or age.

Thank you very much and looking forward to other cooperation.

Best regards

Prof. MVDr.
                    Rector

Univerzita veterinárskeho lekárstva
v Košiciach
Komenského 73, 041 81 Košice$_2$

-mail: rektor@uvm.sk
ttp://www.uvm.sk

Tel: +421/55/633 21 11-15, 633 90 14
         +421/55/633 01 27 (Rector's Office)
Fax: +421/55/632 36 66
         +421/55/633 56 41 (Rector's Fax)

Bank contact: 7000072110/8180
Office treasury
IČO: 397 474
DIČ: 397 474/695

SAMIR KEBAB CENTER

The glory of kebab

Hi

Thanks for your letter and your interest in Samir Kebab center. I hope we will both be satisfied with our future business collaboration.

Samir Kebab center buys all sorts of animals, with the exception of pigs. However, Samir Kebab center buys all other forms of animals. We are especially interested in small birds and other smaller-sized animals, for example, rodents, which after processing can be sold as chicken kebabs. We pay 5 USD per 10 kilo of small animals, larger animals go for 4 USD per 10 kilo. The rates are of course open to negotiation. Which kinds animals do you have available for sale and in what quantities? I also wanted to know if it would be possible to pick up the first delivery in the middle of March?

Best regards,

Eric Ericson

UNIVERSITY OF VETERINARY MEDICINE IN KOŠICE
Komenského 73, 041 81 Košice, Slovak Republic

Košice, 03.03.2006
Č.j.: 172/R/2006

Eric Ericson
Samir Kebab Center
Mailbox 412
Birger Jarlsgatan 39
111 45 Stockholm
Sweden

Dear Mr. Ericson.

On the basis of your letter, that you are interesting in buying animals, we would like to confirm our willingnis to be in contact with you.
We are producing mainly pigs, beef and the ship. The price, which you offer is to low (the prices on our market are: pigs 50,- to 60,- Sk, it is approximately 2 USD / kg and beef 3 USD / kg). So, if the price would be like that or better, we could cooperate.

Best regards

Prof. MVDr.
Rector

Univerzita veterinárskeho lekárstva
v Košiciach
Komenského 73, 041 81 Košice₂

E-mail: rektor@uvm.sk   Tel: +421/55/633 21 11-15, 633 90 14   Bank contact: 7000072110/8180
                                      +421/55/633 01 27 (Rector's Office)   Office treasury
http://www.uvm.sk   Fax: +421/55//632 36 66   IČO: 397 474
                                      +421/55/633 56 41 (Rector's Fax)   DIČ: 397 474/695

Dear Sir or Madam

My name is Eric Ericson and I have read on the internet that you add various narcotic ingredients, such as heroine, cocaine and morphine to your products to add an addiction to your products. In my opinion, this is both good and bad. I find it frightening that people become addicted to your products, it is as immoral as selling drugs. The advantage is that people buy lots of snacks, which creates job opportunities and gives tax flow which builds our country and the army. I like your products and I wonder if you have any products that do not contain narcotic ingredients or other substances that stimulate the central nervous system. Until I receive a reply from you I will not eat any of your products.

Kindly regards

Eric Ericson
Mailbox 412
Birger Jarlsgatan 39
111 45 Stockoholm
Sweden

WORLD HEADQUARTERS

600 Grant Street
Pittsburgh, Pennsylvania 15219-2857

December 19, 2005

Mr. Eric Ericson
Mailbox 412
Birger Jarlsgatan 39
111 45 Stockholm
Sweden

Dear Mr. Ericson:

I am writing to you regarding your recent correspondence about the H. J. Heinz Company and its products.

I can assure you that we do not add any narcotic ingredients to our products. Heinz has a long history of quality dating back to the 1800's when our founder put horseradish in a clear jar so that consumers could see that it was unadulterated. In addition, Heinz was instrumental in the passage of the first Pure Food and Drug Act in 1906. We still abide by the same principles.

I hope this response allays your concerns and that you can once again enjoy Heinz products.

Very truly yours,

AF SILVERHUFVUD

Dear Sir

I'm contacting you on behalf of the Silverhufvud family. Since the previous fall the family has allowed a person belonging to you to live on the estate. The man was found in the Silverhufvud family orchard attempting to steal fallen fruit late in the season.

He was first permitted to stay in the gate house, but when he later stole all the brass knobs from the door handles, he was moved to the stables. The man claims to be Thomas Ohlsson and according to him he works at your office as a clerk. He looks to be about 55-65 years of age but claims to be 30 years old and a descendent of the Tsar. He doesn't speak, but communicates with handwritten notes. The Silverhufvud family has enjoyed the company of this strange guest, but have now decided to allow him to return to his rightful owners. We plan to return the person to you the 16th of April. If the delivery address is something other than this one, please send word of the correct address at the earliest convenience. If you have any further questions please do not hesitate to contact me.

Yours sincerely,

Eric Ericson

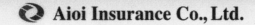

Aioi Insurance Co., Ltd.

March 22, 2006

Mr. Eric Ericson
AF Silverhufvud
Mailbox 412, Birger Jarlsgatan 39
111 45 Stockholm
Sweden

Dear Mr. Ericson:

We have received your letter sent on February 27, 2006, requesting a sending address of a man named 'Thomas Ohlsson', claiming to be a clerk of our company.

I have checked all of our employees, not only our company, but also all of our subsidiaries, affiliates, and agents for a 'Thomas Ohlsson'.   As a result, I regret to inform you that we do not have a 'Thomas Ohlsson' in our company.

According to the investigation result, Thomas Ohlsson does not belong to our company, so unfortunately, we cannot accept his arrival to our firm.   I hope that you could find his rightful owner soon and send him back to where he belongs.

If you have any questions, please feel free to contact me.

Sincerely yours,

Assistant Manager
International Department
Aioi Insurance Co., Ltd.

Aioi Insurance Co., Ltd.
1-28-1,Ebisu,Shibuya-ku,Tokyo 150-8488,Japan

Dear Sir or Madam

About three weeks ago I washed my niece's dog with shampoo from your company. The shampooing went delightfully and the dog really seemed to like the shampoo, which I appreciated very much. But that's not the reason for this letter. One week after the shampooing the dog started to foam at the mouth and behave extremely aggressively, which he'd never done before. A week after that, the dog had died. I am convinced that the death of the dog is a direct consequence of the shampooing. I therefore demand an explanation from you. As a consumer I also demand that you have some kind of warning label on your products that clearly inform that dogs should NOT be washed with your shampoo products, exactly like the warning labels on cigarettes that say its dangerous to smoke.

Regards,

Eric Ericson
Mailbox 412
Birger Jarlsgatan 39
111 45 Stockholm
Sweden

February 6, 2006

Mr. Eric Ericson
Mailbox 412
Birger Jarlsgatan 39
111 45 Stockholm Sweden

Dear Mr. Ericson:

Thank you for taking the time to write to us and for allowing us to address your concerns.
We certainly regret to hear of the loss of your niece's pet, and we do understand your distress.

Please be assured that all Bumble and bumble products are extensively researched and
evaluated and must pass stringent product performance requirements before being approved
for distribution, among them consumer safety, efficacy, product compatibility, convenience, and
durability. Skin and hair requirements of humans can vary from skin, hair or fur requirements of
animals. Therefore, it is always prudent to use products that are specifically formulated for
animal use on animals.

Nonetheless, we do not believe there is anything contained in any of our shampoos that could
cause either the condition you describe that occurred one week after shampooing the dog, or
the dog's death the following week. We do believe there were other causative circumstances
involved, and we suggest that you discuss this matter with your veterinarian, who is in the best
position to evaluate all of the factors involved. We would be happy to provide you with the
ingredients list for the product for your veterinarian's review, if you would let us know the exact
name of the shampoo that was used.

We trust this information will put your mind at ease, and we hope you will continue to look to
Bumble and bumble for all you hair care needs.

Sincerely,

Executive Director
Global Consumer Communications

2,286,662

Dear ██████

I've been in contact with you previously regarding a dog which had passed away after having been shampooed with one of your products. Recently, I shampooed another dog with the same kind of shampoo. That animal didn't die after using your product. Do you think I took an unnecessary risk when i washed the dog with your shampoo? Or did I do the right thing? How great a risk is it that a dog dies from your shampoo?

Kindly regards,

Eric Ericson
Mailbox 412
Birger Jarlsgatan 39
111 45 Stockoholm
Sweden

May 5, 2006

Mr. Eric Ericson
Mailbox 412
Birger Jarlsgatan 39
111 45 Stockholm Sweden

Dear Mr. Ericson:

Thank you for contacting us once again.

With respect to your query, my letter dated February 6, 2006 indicated our position. We recommend that you speak to a veterinarian regarding your concerns and follow his/her advice.

Sincerely,

Executive Director
Global Consumer Communications

2,286,662

Dear Sir or Madam

The purpose of this letter is to address a very alarming development within Europe. Today, not one of the European Parliaments 625 members has any background as pantomime artist or is working actively within pantomime theater. There are presently no pantomime artists in any of the higher positions in society which is a clear threat to democracy. Not a single pantomime artist sits today in any countries' government within the EU. There aren't any pantomime artists found in any meaningful posts in industry either. This is discrimination, pure and simple. One can easily draw the connection to South Africa during the apartheid regime. If pantomime artists don't get the chance to come into the higher positions within EU and in industry, the oppression of this group is likely to continue. That's why we insist that a change in legislation take place. We demand that a new law be put in place so that even mime artists are allowed to be in on the process of making important decisions and influencing society. The solution is a quota system that makes it so that mime artists get in to high positions in society and in committees. We demand that the inquiry immediately be considered in the European Council and a solution to the problem be put into effect before the turn of the year 2006/2007.

Kindly regards

Eric Ericson
Mailbox 412
Birger Jarlsgatan 39
111 45 Stockoholm
Sweden

EUROPEAN PARLIAMENT

CORRESPONDENCE WITH CITIZENS UNIT

A/641
GA/cns

101725   30.01.2006

Mr. Eric Ericson
Mailbox 412
Birger Jarlsgatan 39

S - 111 45 <u>STOCKHOLM</u>

Dear Sir,

I refer to your letter on the subject of your call for an "active participation of pantomime artists in the political, legislative and decisional process in Europe".

We thank you for your letter, which we read with interest. Please be advised that your comments were noted and we shall refer your suggestions to the competent authorities.

Best wishes for success in your endeavours.

Yours sincerely,

Head of Division

Scotland tourism information

My wife and I are planning a trip to Scotland this summer. There are many things in the culture to entice us, but also the sunshine and shorelines. We have a number of acquaintances who have visited the area and have been very pleased. There is just one thing we are worried about. Is it entirely safe to travel to Scotland? We read on the Internet that many people who have been to Scotland have been abducted by UFOs. That is very terrifying. We would like to know how many have suffered from this and how great a risk is it that something like this would happen? We want to know if there are certain areas where this is more prevalent than others? We also want to take the opportunity to ask if there are any special places you think visitors to Scotland shouldn't miss while visiting Scotland?

Thank you,

Eric Ericson
Mailbox 412
Birger Jarlsgatan 39
111 45 Stockoholm
Sweden

visit**scotland**.com
The Official Site of Scotland's National Tourism Board

Our ref: DT070406

Mr Eric Ericson
Mailbox 412
Birger Jarlsgatan 39
Stockholm
Sweden

Dear Mr Ericson

Thank you for contacting **visitscotland.com**

I have requested a selection of Scottish Brochures are sent to your address in Sweden.

We are unaware of any visitors to Scotland being abducted by UFO's or aliens. We cannot comment on any claims that this has happened in Ireland, however, The Irish Tourist Board may be able to offer you further advice. As to your question regarding prevalent areas for this type of activity, again we are unaware of instances of abduction.

The Bonnybridge area near Falkirk in Central Scotland is known as a hotspot for UFO sightings though no proof or findings have substantiated these claims.

Kind regards

visitscotland.com

Fairways Business Park
Deer Park Avenue
Livingston
EH54 8AF Scotland

Telephone: +44 (0)1506 832 100
Facsimile: +44 (0)1506 832 111
Booking Centre: 0845 22 55 121

Email: info@visitscotland.com
Web: visitscotland.com

Dear ████████

Thanks for your letter and brochures. What a relief to hear that it isn't dangerous to be in Scotland. There certainly are many attractions that entice us to come to Scotland. I have a question concerning safety in Scotland. Some say that the best thing to do is run if a UFO comes, others say to stand still. How do you think we should react if a UFO comes this summer?

Kindly regards

Eric Ericson
Mailbox 412
Birger Jarlsgatan 39
111 45 Stockoholm
Sweden

visitscotland.com

The Official Site of Scotland's National Tourism Board

Our ref: DT070406

Mr Eric Ericson
Mailbox 412
Birger Jarlsgatan 39
Stockholm
Sweden

Dear Mr Ericson

Thank you for contacting **visitscotland.com**

As I had stated in my previous letter visitscotland.com are unaware of any visitors to Scotland being abducted by UFO's or aliens and therefore we are unsure of how one should react to an encounter with an alien from a UFO.

You may wish to contact some experts in this field who will be able to give you an insight into alien behaviour and how one should react if they should find themselves in a predicament. A good starting point for you may be to log on to the website http://www.ufomagazine.co.uk/ on this website they have a forum where other parties worldwide exchange information about UFO's. The forum can be reached direct at weblink http://www.ufomagazine.co.uk/wforum/default.asp.

We wish you a wonderful and memorable trip should you come to visit Scotland in the near future.

Kind regards

visitscotland.com

Fairways Business Park
Deer Park Avenue
Livingston
EH54 8AF Scotland

Telephone: +44 (0)1506 832 100
Facsimile: +44 (0)1506 832 111
Booking Centre: 0845 22 55 121

Email: info@visitscotland.com
Web: visitscotland.com

Regarding the mime train.

After the fall of the Soviet Union, 1600 soldiers and border guards were entered into a compulsory reeducation program to become mime dancers in order to solve the occupation crisis and unemployment problem. These mime dancers today form a part of a special clan of mimes. Every other year, the clan departs by train from Bucharest and heads west. This year, the mime train will establish a temporary base in Switzerland between May 27 and August 11. The clan of mimes are financed by various former Eastern European states as well as from EU subsidies. A preliminary stage and camp will be established near your office. We are going to need to set up a canteen at your office between May 27 and August 11 to provide nourishment for the mimes, as well access to running water, WC and showers for the mimes. We therefore need access to your office 7 days a week during the time of our stay. If you are not able to participate, you need to contact the representative below at the latest 4 weeks before the mime trains departure.

Kindly Regards

National Mime Center for the people.
Mailbox 412
Birger Jarlsgatan 39
111 45 Stockoholm
Sweden

National Mime Center for the people
Mailbox 412
Birger Jarlsgatan 39
111 45 Stockholm
Sweden

April 12, 2006

To whom it may concern

This is to inform you that we are unable to participate in the activities mentioned in your undated and unsigned notice posted in Sweden on 04/09/2006.

Sincerely,

Gesellschaft der Freunde des
Weizmann Institute of Science

Regarding invitation

This past Christmas, I attended a Christian Conference and met a person who worked at your of-
fiice. He was very pleasant and we spoke to each
other about Jesus. I told him that I own a lot of
animals. He then told me that he also likes animals and that many people at your company are very
fond of animals. He invited me to come to your office and wanted me to stay for about two weeks with
all of my animals. I have a truck loaded with tons
of animals. I usually release the animals in the
office so that all the office employees can be involved in helping catch the animals again. Sometimes it takes a few days to find the smallest ones.
We'll recapture the animals that are angry with
nets. I just wanted to say that I'm going to be in
the area, so I thought I'd come over March 23th
with the animals. If anyone is allergic, it would
be a good idea for them to be on another floor when
I let loose the animals. If you would rather that I
come in the summer, you need to contact me before I
leave town in my truck.

Eric Ericson
Mailbox 412
Birger Jarlsgatan 39
111 45 Stockoholm
Sweden Sweden

BSL

Banchieri dal 1873

Milano, 02/03/2006

Dear Mr Ericson,

We have received your letter, unfortunately we cannot have strangers in our bank. We are

a Private Banking, we receive high-level clients every day and it's not possible to look

after and catch your animals.

Therefore due to the security reasons we cannot have animals or people running around

our building because we have very sophisticated alarm system.

We are very sorry for the misunderstanding, probably the person you have spoken with

has underestimate all the logistic problems.

Yours faithfully

Banca BSI Italia S.pA.

ca **BSI Italia S.pA.** - Sede Legale: Piazza S.Alessandro 4, 20123 Milano - Società unipersonale - Tel. 02 88552.1 - Fax 02 88558810 - E-mail: milano@bsi.it - Web site: www.bsi.it
Capitale Sociale: € 9.288.000 i.v. - R.E.A. Milano 1217105 - Codice Fiscale ed iscrizione Registro Imprese Milano 01129040281 - Partita IVA 08338110151
Iscrizione all'Albo delle Banche Nr. 5513 - Codice ABI 3209.4 - CAB 1600.6 - SWIFT: BSILTMM
Aderente al Fondo Interbancario di Tutela dei Depositi e al Fondo Nazionale di Garanzia

Dear Sir

I'm contacting you on behalf of the Silverhufvud family. Since the previous fall the family has allowed a person belonging to you to live on the estate. The man was found in the Silverhufvud family orchard attempting to steal fallen fruit late in the season.

He was first permitted to stay in the gate house, but when he later stole all the brass knobs from the door handles, he was moved to the stables. The man claims to be Thomas Ohlsson and according to him he works at your office as a clerk. He looks to be about 55-65 years of age but claims to be 30 years old and a descendent of the Tsar. He doesn't speak, but communicates with handwritten notes. The Silverhufvud family has enjoyed the company of this strange guest, but have now decided to allow him to return to his rightful owners. We plan to return the person to you the 16th of April. If the delivery address is something other than this one, please send word of the correct address at the earliest convenience. If you have any further questions please do not hesitate to contact me.

Yours sincerely,

Eric Ericson

March 3, 2006

Dear Mr. Ericson:

I refer to your letter("Letter") undated but provided on behalf of Silvferhufvud family, which we received yesterday.

As it seems that we do not have any acquaintance at all with either Silvferhufvud family or the gentleman you referred to in the Letter as long as being based upon the information as provided therein, we cannot stand in a position to accept his being returned toward us and rather appreciate you would seek other possible addressees for taking care of this matter.

Please also note that we of course will not be in a position to bear any disbursement which you may incur in relation to this matter, including but not limited to any travel or accommodation expenses incurred by the gentleman.

Regards,

General Manager

AF SILVFERHUFVUD

Dear Sir or Madam

I'm contacting you on behalf of the Af Silvferhufvud family. The family has been in possession of a dwarf since the 1970's.

The dwarf has given the family much happiness and has been much appreciated by the family's children, friends and relatives.

He has been the family's mascot ever since he was first obtained. The children have now outgrown the dwarf and he's starting to get on in years. We have therefore decided to donate the dwarf to a zoo so more people are able to get some joy out of this little creature. In Sweden the constitution does not permit zoos to be in possession of dwarfs, that is why we have chosen to contact you. The dwarf will be delivered to you February 21. If you have anything against this arrangement we ask you to get in touch with us immediately so we can contact a different zoo. We would like to thank you in advance for your help and at the same time wish you the best with our little friend. If you have any questions don't hesitate to ask.

Yours sincerely,

Eric Ericson

Egypt

Ministry of agriculture
and land reclamation

General veterinary services

Central Administration of
Egyptian Zoos and Wild Life

Dear Eric Ericson

I was happy when I received your letter, it was a good surprise to read
that you decided to donate the dwarf (your Little friend) to our zoo.
Before I accept your decision, I need from you to give us a short notes
about your little friend (dwarf's life, feeding, all his certificates and
information about him). It is good to send a recent picture for him to
us, also I want to tell us about the cost of transportation and (either
you will pay or us), I hope that you will answer all my questions very
fast, for prepare our self to say welcome for the dwarf and accept your
decision or not.

Thank you very much

Yours sincerely

Dr ▮▮▮▮▮▮▮▮▮▮

Under secretary of state for
Egyptian Zoos and Wild life

Dear Sir or Madam

I have a question. For many years I drank coffee daily. I've stopped drinking coffee after many years as a coffee-drinker. Not because its too expensive, but because many say it isn't healthy. I've started smoking coffee instead. I wonder if it is just as dangerous to smoke coffee as it is to drink coffee? Or are they both just as dangerous? I don't smoke tobacco and never have because of health risks. It was because of health risks that I stopped drinking coffee. Actually, I don't even really like smoking coffee, but it's an obsession. I've looked for information about this on your website, but they didn't say anything about it. I have even looked for information on the internet about it without success. I would be grateful of you could answer these questions as soon as possible.

Kindly regards

Eric Ericson
Mailbox 412
Birger Jarlsgatan 39
111 45 Stockoholm
Sweden

CoSIC

*Coffee Science
Information
Centre*

12 Market Street, Chipping Norton, OX7 5NQ
Tel: (+44) 1608 645566 • Fax: (+44) 1608 645300
E-mail: CoSIC@BTInternet.com • Web: www.cosic.org

Eric Ericson
Mailbox 412
Birger Jarlsgatan 39
111 45 Stockholm
SWEDEN

5th December 2005

Dear Mr Ericson

Thank you for your recent enquiry regarding your smoking coffee. I am afraid that we do not have any scientific papers that cover this subject and are therefore unable to help you.

I would stress that coffee is one of the most heavily researched products in the world today and coffee drinking in moderation is perfectly safe.

With kind regards

Director

Regarding the Exchange Program

On February **23** th, **17** Rumanian laborers will arrive at your place of business to bake bread. The purpose of this exchange program is to create closer con-
nections between workers in the European Union and the
former eastern block countries. You will be compensat-
ed with 1 Euro per person, per work day. The project
will continue for 7 months. The project is implemented
and financed by a variety of EU entities, national
cooperatives, departments within a variety of sec-
tors and certain local factions within the EU in collaboration with the former eastern block states. If
you aren't able to participate, you must contact the
project leader below at the latest 4 weeks before the
project's start date. We would also like to take the
opportunity to thank you for being a part of the European Union.

Regards

EU Center for national workforce exchange,
Northern Office
Mailbox 412
Birger Jarlsgatan 39
111 45 Stockoholm
Sweden

QUALITY
BAKERY & PATISSERIE LTD

FLOURISH

Mr Eric Ericson
EU Centre for National Workforce Exchange
Northern Office
Mailbox 412
Birger Jarlsgatan 39
111 45 Stockholm
Sweden

16th January 2006

Dear Mr Ericson

I am writing to inform you that I am unable to participate in your
Romanian exchange programme.
We simply do not have the facilities nor the work to engage 17 bakers.

Yours truly,

Miss Helen O'Connell

Dear Sir or Madam

Enclosed within is the plaing card and the money as per agreement.
Please send the prize to the address below.

Kindly regards

Eric Ericson
Mailbox 412
Birger Jarlsgatan 39
111 45 Stockoholm
Sweden

OREGON LOTTERY®

It does good things™

April 11, 2006

Eric Ericson
Mailbox 412
Birger Jarlsgatan 39
111 45 Stockholm
SWEDEN

Dear Mr. Ericson:

Thank you for your interest in the Oregon Lottery. I am not sure what "agreement" you refer to in your letter. However, Oregon Lottery tickets must be purchased in person at a retail location in Oregon. We do net sell our games through the mail or over the Internet.

We are enclosing the playing card and the 1 Yuan that you sent us through the mail.

Sincerely,

Dear ███████

Thank you for your letter. I talked with Roger who originally told me that I should send the playing card and the 1 Yuan to you. He told me that I should return the playing card and the 1 Yuan, along with a penalty-fee of 20 USD for not having returned the card before the turn of the new year. If I didn't, I would be obligated to pay the prize amount to the next lotto winner and that would be financially unfeasible for me. He also said that I should request a receipt from you to show that you've received the money.

Kindly regards

Eric Ericson
Mailbox 412
Birger Jarlsgatan 39
111 45 Stockoholm
Sweden

OREGON LOTTERY

May 2, 2006

It does good things™

Eric Ericson
Mailbox 412
Birger Jarlsgatan 39
111 45 Stockholm
SWEDEN

Dear Mr. Ericson:

On April 12, 2006, we received your second letter containing a single playing card. Your third letter, containing one playing card, one Yuan, and a US $20 bill, arrived today.

Roger, the individual you spoke with, is not affiliated with the Oregon Lottery, and the activity he described is not part of any Oregon Lottery game. The contest or drawing that you mentioned is not offered or operated by our lottery. There are some individuals and organizations that simply use the address of an actual lottery or sweepstakes in order to make their organization appear to be legitimate. We urge you to do thorough research on any individual or party before sending any money. It is very possible that you will lose your money and receive nothing in return.

We are returning the playing cards, one Yuan, and the $20.00 bill that you included in your letters. In the future, please do not send any money or playing cards to the Oregon Lottery. If you wish to play our games, you will need to visit a retail location in our state and purchase tickets in person.

Sincerely,

Marl
Publ

San Marino tourism information

A friend of mine has just been to San Marino was really pleased with the trip. He told me that it was all right to use color-copied money. Are color-copiers available there? Or should the bills be color-copied before travel? My friend said that it was possible to color-copy money at the tourist information office. I wonder if that service is available in every tourist information office or just at certain ones? Or do you know some place where money can be color-copied for even cheaper?

I would also appreciate it if you could send a few brochures.

Best regards,

Eric Ericson
Mailbox 412
Birger Jarlsgatan 39
111 45 Stockoholm
Sweden

Repubblica di San Marino
Ufficio di Stato per il Turismo

Prot. 00998 - 18/4/2006 - 21-02
Rif. V-1/PM/GL

San Marino li, 18 aprile 2006/1705 d.F.R.

ERIC ERICSON
Mailbox 412
Birger Jarlsgatan 39
111 45 Stockholm
<u>SVEZIA</u>

Dear Mr. Ericson,

With reference to your letter about color-copied money in San Marino, we inform you that we do not know anything about this matter.

Here you can use euros like in other European countries; if you want to buy San Marino's euros you must ask to the Numismatic office in Piazza Garibaldi or in some tourist shops in the historical centre.

We send you enclosed some tourist literature about our country.

With best regards.

Sincerely,

Managing Director

ntrada Omagnano, 20 - 47890 Repubblica di San Marino A-1 - Tel. 0549 882400 - 0549 882410 - Fax 0549 882575 - International area code (+)378 - E-Mail: statoturismo@omniway.sm

CIRCUS MARXISM

I own a small circus consisting of my brother, a dozen animals and myself. We are not an ordinary circus, but a political circus. Circus Marxism spreads a political message to the people. You don't have to pay o go to Circus Marxism. That's how Marx would have liked it to be. Circus Marxism is always on the road, performing to reach as many as possible. We are proud to be one of the few Marxist circuses remaining after the fall of the Soviet Union. To go to Circus Marxism is free of charge, and that's the reason why we do not have any money. That's the reason why we can't stay in a hotel. We would really appreciate if we could stay in one of your conference rooms as we're coming to Birmingham. The concerned period would be January 12 to February 7, when we continue on our journey to Palestine. That would be great. You only need to respond to this letter, if for some reason we can't stay at your place. Otherwise we'll just see each other in January .

Take care

Eric Ericson
Mailbox 412
Birger Jarlsgatan 39
111 45 Stockoholm
Sweden

Industrie- und Handelskammer Frankfurt am Main, 60284 Frankfurt

Circus Marxism
Mr. Eric Ericson
Mailbox 412
Birger Jarlsgatan 39
111 45 Stockholm
SCHWEDEN

Ihr Zeichen, Ihre Nachricht vom	Unser Zeichen, unsere Nachricht vom	Telefon	Frankfurt am Main
	ÖA/MM-ST		05-11-30

Dear Mr. Ericson,

thank you for your letter of 2. November 2005. We are sorry to inform you that we have
to reject your inquiry to stay at the Frankfurt am Main Chamber of Commerce and
Industry.

The CCI Frankfurt am Main is a public law corporation and we are subject of strict
security regulations. Our conference rooms are used to arrange events, exhibitions and
other kinds of activities.

Kind regards

Chamber of Commerce and Industry
Frankfurt am Main
Corporate Communications

i.V.

Deputy Director

Hausanschrift:	Postanschrift:	Telefon: 069 2197-0
IHK Frankfurt am Main	IHK Frankfurt am Main	Telefax: 069 2197-1488
Börsenplatz 4	60284 Frankfurt	s.stallknecht@frankfurt-main.ihk.de
60313 Frankfurt		www.frankfurt-main.ihk.de

Czech Republic tourism information

A friend of mine has just been to Czech was really pleased with the trip. He told me that it was all right to use color-copied money. Are color-copiers available there? Or should the bills be color-copied before travel? My friend said that it was possible to color-copy money at the tourist information office. I wonder if that service is available in every tourist information office or just at certain ones? Or do you know some place where money can be color-copied for even cheaper?

I would also appreciate it if you could send a few brochures.

Best regards,

Eric Ericson
Mailbox 412
Birger Jarlsgatan 39
111 45 Stockoholm
Sweden

Česká republika

Mr. Eric Ericsson
Mailbox 412
Birger Jarlsgatan 39
111 45 Stockholm
Sweden

Prague, 20th April 2006

Dear Mr. Ericson,

Czech Tourist Authority – CzechTourism has received your letter telling us that a friend of yours was all right to use color-copied money in the Czech Republic. Your friend also said that it was possible to color-copy money at an tourist Information office. Could you, please, write us the address of that Tourist Information Office?
Copying money is illegal and we would like to inform office of the Czech Police.
You will get some brochures about the Czech Republic per post.

Best regards

manažer TIC

Česká centrála cestovního ruchu - CzechTourism
Vinohradská 46
120 41 Praha 2
e-mail: info@czechtourism.cz
tel: +420 221580611
www.czechtourism.com
www.czechtourism.cz

Bilderna på följande sidor är hämtade ur boken
Brev till Clara och Tyra från Eric Ericson,
Kartago förlag, 2009.

KORVER, HÄSTER, PLUTO OCH MISTER
I FÖLJD. NÄVER ÅTTA TAR RÄVER SJU.
DU ÄR SKYLDIG LÄNSMAN OCH SVERKER
SJUTTIO KRONOR VARDERA.

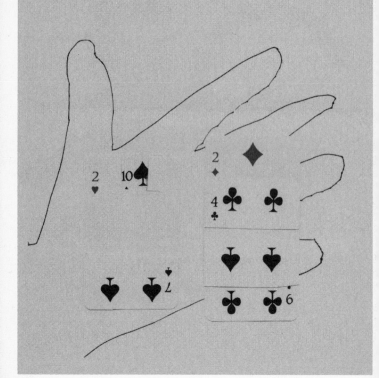

JAG ÄR MARJA. JAG SYNS INTE,
OCH JAG FINNS INTE I TRADITIONEL
MENING. JAG ÄR ETT OFFER
PÅ GRUND AV DE REGLER SOM
FINNS. JAG KOMMER INTE IN
GENOM   PÄRLEPORTEN
OCH   JAG   HAR INTE
HELLER   TILLGÅNG TILL
MIN LÄGENHET   I BANDHAGEN.
JAG HAR   FASTNAT
MELLAN   TVÅ BYRÅKRATISKA
SYSTEM. JAG ÄR DJÄVLIGT
BESVIKEN. JAG ÄR FAN
FÖRBANNAD PÅ ALLT.
SPECIELLT PÅ MÄN.
FAN TA TOBIAS!

Till samtliga kunder

Vi är bara sex man kvar om räknar bort Anneli som vi håller
isolerad efter hennes upprepade stölder av trisslotter. Sex man
är för lite för att driva den form av livsmedelbutik som vi gör.
Vi är alltså kraftigt underbemannade. Att anställa fler är inte
aktuellt av flera anledningar. En anledning är att det skulle
innebära högre priser för slutkonsumenten. Ytterligare en
anledning är det kan vara svårt för en ny person att komma in i
den starka sammanhållning vi har på Konsum i Kristineberg. Det
finns också en risk för att en ny person skulle skapa
splittringar i gruppen och förstöra allt vi har byggt upp. Det
skulle dessutom ta mycket lång tid för en ny person att lära sig
alla sånger vi sjunger på morgonmötet. Så därför har vi valt att
inte nyanställa.

Hälsningar

Björn Hansson

Personalansvarig och skyddsombud,
Konsum Kristineberg

Till samtligt boende i Kristineberg

Anneli har rymt. Anneli har svikit sig själv, gruppen, sin heder
och samtidigt förstört chansen att rehabiliteras.
Detta är mycket allvarligt. Så allvarligt att vi för första
gången på ett decennium inte sjöng någon sång på morgonmötet.
Vi uppmanar boende i området runt Konsum Kristineberg att
omedelbart kontakta oss om ni har sett Anneli eller har
upplysningar om var hon kan befinna sig. Anneli kan vara oerhört
aggressiv och vi uppmanar boende att inte själva ingripa. Den
som har upplysningar som leder till ett gripande av Anneli
kommer belönas med ett presentkort på 300 kr.

Hälsningar

Björn Hansson

Personalansvarig och skyddsombud,
Konsum Kristineberg

Information till boende i Konsum Kristinebergs närområde.

Anneli har fortfarande inte återfunnits. På Konsum i
Kristineberg har inte heller fått in enda tips. Vi tycker att
det är märkligt att inte ett enda tips har kommit in. Rimligtvis
borde någon sett henne. Vi misstänker att boende i Kristineberg
undanhåller information. Vi har därför valt att införa
sanktioner tills tips kommer in. Från och med lördag kommer vi
sluta sälja bröd och mejeriprodukter tills tips börjar komma in.
Vi tycker det känns tråkigt att många boende i Kristineberg
drabbas av detta men vi ser detta som nödvändigt i kampen mot
brottslighet.

Tips kan ringas in dygnet runt.

Hälsningar

Björn Hansson

Personalansvarig och skyddsombud,
Konsum Kristineberg